Date: 6/16/20

641.5676 ALF
Alfond, Kenden,
Feeding women of the Bible,
feeding ourselves : uplifting

FEEDING WOMEN OF THE BIBLE, FEEDING OURSELVES

FEEDING WOMEN OF THE BIBLE, FEEDING OURSELVES

Uplifting the Voices of Hebrew Biblical Heroines and Honoring Them with Simple, Plant-Based Recipes

by Kenden Alfond

JEWISH FOOD HERO

Nourishing your mind,

body, and spirit

All scripture is from *The Hebrew Bible: A Translation and Commentary* by Robert Alter unless otherwise stated.

Turner Publishing Company
Nashville, Tennessee
www.turnerpublishing.com

Cover design: Rachel Mendelson
Book design: Rachel Mendelson
Photography: Sonja Lazukic Silly World Photography

Library of Congress Cataloging-in-Publication Data Available Upon Request

9781684423262 Paperback
9781684423279 Hardcover
9781684423286 Ebook

Printed in the United States of America
17 18 19 20 10 9 8 7 6 5 4 3 2 1

To the women in my family:

my grandmothers, Bibby and Ellen;
my mother, Joan;
and my daughter, Yael

TABLE OF CONTENTS

INTRODUCTION

For many of us, Jewish food is intertwined with memory, our personal history, our family and our Jewish heritage. This is all true *and* I am just as interested in what Jewish people are feeding themselves and their children *now*. I want to know how we are honouring our Jewish traditions, our personal preferences and our health by our food choices.

When I was preparing recipes for Purim 2018, I was living in rural Cambodia. I created a high protein black bean brownie Hamantaschen recipe inspired by Asian bean desserts. Although I liked the recipe, focusing on making a cookie inspired by the story's main antagonist somehow missed the mark for what I wanted to achieve with food that Purim.

Esther, the heroine of Purim, is not represented when the food we prepare focuses on the Haman. In a moment of inspiration, I had the idea of creating a plant-based Purim dish specifically to honour Esther. This recipe was a moment when several points joined together on my path as a Jewish woman working with, and eating, plant-based food. In this day and age, with all the produce available to us and all the knowledge we have about the impact of our food choices, is it really necessary for us to focus our ceremonial eating on cookies? Who can feel good when they do?

Making healthy food specifically for Esther gave me a sense that there was something more meaningful about cooking for the holiday. This process enabled me to direct prolonged attention on one particular female character in the Hebrew Bible, deepening my knowledge of her story and, in doing so, creating a connection with her. As a result, both the process and the product of cooking became more nourishing.

This first recipe, "Esther's Nourishing Grain Bowl" (you can see it below in this introduction section), is the seed from which this book grew. The result is this collection of chapters, each devoted to one female biblical character followed by two healthy plant-based recipes created specifically for her.

I chose 20 women who had significant roles in the Hebrew Bible, who embody traits that are inspirational to me personally and who I think will inspire women everywhere.

HOW THIS COOKBOOK IS ORGANIZED[1]

This community cookbook is the co-creation of Jewish women, with biblical narratives contributed by Rabbis, Rabbinical students, Jewish teachers and emerging thought leaders. Recipe contributions come from professional chefs with decades of experience and homecooks who are elementary school students and great-grandmothers.

The book is organized by chapters. Each chapter is devoted to one female character from the Hebrew Bible and has the following sections:

Story: a concise summary of the female biblical character's narrative.

Verses: key quotations from the Hebrew Bible relating to the biblical character's narrative. All quotations are from *The Hebrew Bible: A Translation and Commentary* by Robert Alter. For page numbers of specific verses, please see the Reference section.

Themes: essential emotional, mental, physical, social themes that define the character's narrative or role.

Midrash: a modern commentary, uplifting the voice of the biblical woman without attempting to neutralise her imperfections, flaws or struggles.

Prompts: meaningful questions arising from the story, to inspire further reflection for women today.

Food Offerings: two plant-based recipes, each developed as an offering to, inspired by and to honour the female biblical character.

---

1. Please also see the section "A Note on Inclusion"

HOW TO USE THIS COOKBOOK

As a traditional cookbook

Dip in and out at your leisure, be inspired by new recipes coupled with intellectual and spiritual stimulation to deepen the experience.

As a learning experience

Go at your own pace, work through the book learning about the female biblical characters and enjoy plant-based recipes that might have nourished them.

As a meaningful collective experience

Create a group learning and eating experience by using this book like a book club text. Invite your friends to read a specific female narrative and then cook the recipes together. Think about other recipes which might nourish each biblical character. Use the prompts for reflection as discussion topics to get beyond the small talk which can sometimes dominate our social gatherings.

ABOUT THE RECIPES

The recipes proposed in this book are plant-based and kosher pareve. The recipes center around plant-based foods: fruits, vegetables, starchy vegetables, roots/tubers, intact whole grains, and legumes such as beans, peas and lentils. Many of the recipes are oil-free and the ones that contain oil have a reduced amount

Incorporating more plant-based foods into your regular eating pattern has three primary benefits:

1. Mood and Energy Levels: Eating minimally processed plant-based foods stabilizes how you feel throughout the day.
2. Environmental: Food consumption impacts animals and our environment. In particular, factory farming and other large-scale meat and dairy production contributes to climate change.
3. Disease Prevention: Common health problems that can be prevented or improved by eating a plant-based diet include: diabetes, heart disease, obesity, acne, intestinal diseases, depression, fatigue, liver disease, kidney disease, high blood pressure, and more.

CHARITY

All of the contributors, including me, volunteered their time and intellectual energy to create this book. As such, all of Jewish Food Hero's proceeds from the sale of this book will be donated to a Jewish nonprofit every year.

A FINAL NOTE

Classical Jewish texts were written in a time and place with specific values and norms about gender and sexuality. Some of the ideas and stories from these texts may not resonate with your lived experience and values. Today, the Jewish community holds a wide spectrum of ideas about gender and sexuality. We do not study these narratives to necessarily glean a simplistic prescription for how we should think, feel and act in the world today. We study to settle our mind, refine our character, and to distill the varied texts of our tradition.

The essence of this project is about uplifting the voices of women; women from the Hebrew Bible and Jewish women from our community.

May these female biblical stories and plant-based recipes nourish your body, mind and spirit. I'm so glad you're here.

To your health and inspiration,

Kenden

ESTHER'S NOURISHING GRAIN BOWL

To honor Queen Esther, I created a healthy, nourishing dish.

I find the Talmudic story of Queen Esther's vegetarianism compelling and inspiring. (It appears in some manuscripts of Megillah 13b.) Esther needed to keep the laws of kashrut while hiding her Jewish heritage, so vegetarianism was the perfect solution. Based on what we know today, it's highly possible that her switch to eating more fruits, vegetables, tubers, legumes and whole grains impacted how she felt in her body and in the world.

This delicious quinoa bowl is hearty and satisfying thanks to the plant-protein in the quinoa and lentils. Feel free to switch out the vegetables for whatever you have on hand or anything seasonal and fresh.

Prep time: 10 minutes
Cook time: 20 minutes
Serves: 6

Tools:

- Medium saucepan
- Vegetable peeler
- Box grater or julienne vegetable peeler

Ingredients:

- 1 cup (90 g) quinoa (makes 3 cups cooked)
- 2 cups (500 ml) water
- 1 teaspoon turmeric
- 1 tablespoon lemon juice
- ¼ teaspoon salt
- ¼–½ cup (25–50 g) chopped green onions
- 3 cups (150 g) of julienne shredded carrots
- 3 cups (360) of whole green beans
- 4 tomatoes, chopped
- 1 cup (100 g) of whole pistachios, shelled and roughly chopped
- For the lentils:
- 1 cup (200 g) lentils
- 3 cups (750 ml) vegetable broth or water
- ½ teaspoon cumin powder
- ½ teaspoon coriander powder
- ½ teaspoon salt
- For the tahini dressing:
- 1 tablespoon Tahini
- ½ cup (125 ml) orange juice
- 1 tablespoon rice milk
- 2 tablespoons lemon juice
- 2 garlic cloves
- ¼ teaspoon salt
- Pepper, optional

Instructions:

1. Rinse quinoa and place in a saucepan with 2 cups of water. Bring to a boil, then reduce heat to medium-low and simmer the quinoa for 12–14 minutes.
2. Allow quinoa to cool for 5 minutes in the saucepan, then stir in the turmeric, lemon juice, and chopped green onion; fluff with a fork.
3. While the quinoa is cooking, in a large pot, cook the lentils in the vegetable broth until they are tender, around 15–20 minutes. Season the lentils once cooked as adding salt during cooking can make the lentils tough.
4. While the quinoa and lentils are cooking, steam the green beans until slightly tender, yet still bright green, around 2–3 minutes.
5. Once all components are ready, assemble Esther's nourishing bowls by layering the quinoa and lentils on the bottom of each bowl and topping with the vegetables, nuts, and a dollop of creamy tahini dressing.

From the Jewish Food Hero Kitchen

EVE

STORY

Eve was the first woman. She is part of the creation story that begins the Torah. After God created the heavens and the earth, light and darkness, the land and the seas, and the sun and the stars, God created living creatures. God made animals – of the sea, of the sky, and of the earth – and then God made human beings, called *adam*. God created them, both male and female, in the image of God.

That is one version of how Eve came to be. But the Torah continues with an alternative narrative. God created a human being, the man (literally *ha'adam*), from the soil (*ha'adamah*), and breathed life into his nostrils. God places this man in the Garden of Eden, where the Tree of Life and the Tree of Knowledge of Good and Bad grow. God tells the man he may eat from any tree in the garden, but if he eats from the Tree of Knowledge of Good and Bad, he will die. God declares that it is not good for the man to be alone, and so puts him into a deep sleep, takes part of his body,[1] and forms it into a woman, creating a helpmate for him.

The woman (*ha'isha*) and the man find themselves in the Garden of Eden. A snake hisses to the woman, asking if God really said not to eat from *any* tree? The woman responds that even touching the tree in the middle leads to death. The snake tells her if she eats from this tree, she will become like gods, knowing good and bad. The woman, possibly motivated by desiring knowledge,[2] eats fruit from this tree and gives some to the man. God asks the man and the woman if they have eaten the fruit and they do not deny it, blaming the woman and the snake respectively. God punishes both Adam and Eve, condemning the woman to the anguish of pregnancy and childbirth, and the man to work to grow food from the soil.

It is only after these stories that we learn the woman's name. She is Eve, *Chava*, because she is the mother of all the living. With her husband Adam, Eve gives birth to sons Cain and Abel. Years later, Cain kills Abel in a fit of jealous rage, because God accepted Abel's sacrificial offering but not his. After Abel's death, Eve gives birth to a third son, Seth.

---

1. While the Hebrew word *m'tzalotav* is traditionally translated as 'from his ribs', Tamara Cohn Eskenazi notes that '[t]he word more accurately means "sides," meaning a more substantial part of the *adam*.' Tamara Cohn Eskenazi and Andrea L. Weiss, eds., *The Torah: A Women's Commentary* (New York: URJ Press, 2008), p. 12.
2. Eskenazi notes that the woman's motive 'includes a desire for wisdom.' *The Torah: A Women's Commentary*, p. 14.

VERSES

"And the LORD GOD cast a deep slumber on the human, and he slept, and He took one of his ribs and closed over the flesh where it had been, and the LORD GOD built the rib He had taken from the human into a woman…"

—Genesis 2:21–22

"To the woman He said,
"I will terribly sharpen your birth pangs,
in pain shall you bear children,
And your man shall be your longing,
and he shall rule over you."

—Genesis 3:16

"And the human called his woman's name Eve, for she was the mother of all that lives."

—Genesis 3:20

THEMES

Pioneer

Eve was the first woman, the first wife, the first mother. She pioneered and defined all these roles. While she may have been created from part of Adam's body, she was independent. She chose to eat from the Tree of Knowledge of Good and Bad. She was not forced to do so, although perhaps misled by the snake. She desired the knowledge promised by eating from this tree. Even though Eve was punished for eating the fruit, it was her decision. She had no role models, no other women to follow or look up to. She simply had to be herself.

Vulnerability

Eve is punished for eating the fruit from the tree in the middle of the garden. Adam, her own husband, blames her when God confronts them about eating the fruit. Eve alone is condemned for disobeying God's commands, even though it is the snake who tells her that eating the fruit will cause her eyes to be opened and she will become knowledgeable like gods. Her vulnerability makes her easily influenced and overpowered by others.

Maternity

God breathes Adam into being, yet Eve, like God, is able to create life. Her name *Chava* comes from the Hebrew word for life. Her very being is defined by her ability to give life. Eve gives birth to three sons with Adam: Cain, Abel and Seth. God creates the first man, but Eve creates the second, third and fourth. Eve also experiences a mother's worst nightmare, the death of a child, her son Abel. Her pain is unimaginable. Being able to create life, something so precious, also creates the possibility of losing it. Yet Eve goes on to have another child. Her experience of motherhood is joyous, miraculous and heartbreaking.

MIDRASH

Because she was mother of all living, Rabbi Shimon ben Elazar said that she is with all living.
—*Bereishit Rabbah* 20:11

Eve is a complex figure. She stumbles into the Garden of Eden, a newly created adult woman, her first experience of life a lush, green, divinely created paradise. But she is not alone. In fact, she was created so that the first human, Adam, would not be alone. From the moment she exists, she is Adam's wife, his helpmate, his companion. Eve has no mother. She had no childhood. She did not come into the world a tiny, helpless baby, but a fully grown woman. Eve is not like us. She is not borne of a woman, but created by God.

The Torah tells us that Adam named her Eve because she was *em kol chai*, 'mother of all living'.[1] She represents the ability to create life. Indeed, her name in Hebrew *Chava* shares the same Hebrew root as *chaim* 'life', signifying her capacity to bear children and continue God's creation. Rabbi Shimon ben Elazar, one of our ancient sages, explains that Eve was so named because she is *im kol chai*, 'with all living'.[2] Her gift of creation continues throughout the generations. There is a little bit of Eve in all of us: our ability to create, to create ourselves, to create others, to create a better world.

Eve was a mother, and a wife. Yet there is more to Eve than her traditional family roles. She was also a woman who made her own decisions, and created her own path in life. She was thrown into a world that already had its own rules, and she was punished for breaking them. Perhaps she was

---

1. Genesis 3:20
2. Bereishit Rabbah 20:11

brave, perhaps she was foolish. Perhaps she just made the best decision in the moment and lived with the consequences.

We are all created in God's image. Eve reminds us that we have the power to create others. Let us find the strength to create and recreate ourselves. We each have one life. Eve, giver of life, reminds us of that. Let us embrace the present and remember the preciousness of life. Let us live each day as if it is the only one we have.

PROMPTS

Eve is created in order to be a helpmate to Adam and to create life. She came into being for these very reasons. Has your role in life been pre-defined? How can you work, within the factors which constrain you, to re-define your own role?

Eve loses a child. The Torah does not tell us about Eve's feelings in the aftermath of Abel's death. Perhaps this represents an experience for which there are no words. What experiences have left you lost for words? How do you support others experiencing personal tragedy?

Eve is influenced by the snake, blamed by Adam, and punished by God for eating the fruit. Think of a time when you were influenced and what the consequences were. How do you see this situation now?

Eve's name, *Chava* in Hebrew, describes her very reason for being. How does your name define you? If you could choose, what name would you choose for yourself?

Dr Esther Jilovsky is a rabbinical student at Hebrew Union College, Los Angeles. From Melbourne, Australia, she has a doctorate in German Studies. She is author of Remembering the Holocaust: Generations, Witnessing and Place, writes for the Times of Israel and 929 English, and co-edited In the Shadows of Memory: The Holocaust and the Third Generation. Biblical women's names abound in her family: she is Esther Sarah, her sisters Leah Miriam and Rachel Judith, mother of Hannah, after their Grandma Hanna of blessed memory. She dedicates this piece to them and her mother Cathie, for the many fun times creating yummy food together.

OAT AND CINNAMON APPLE MUFFINS BOWL

The ingredients in these flavorful muffins come from the Garden of Eden. I imagine Adam and Eve picking the ingredients freshly grown and adding them to the muffins. The apples symbolize the fruit of the Tree of Knowledge that Eve bravely picks. (The name of the fruit is not mentioned in the Hebrew Bible and opinions abound as to which fruit it was, but the apple is the most commonly connected with the Tree of Knowledge in contemporary society.)

Perfectly moist and just slightly crumbly, these delicious muffins are bursting with apple goodness in every bite. The oats provide a good dose of fiber and the cinnamon rounds out the muffins with a bit of warm, sweet spice.

Prep time: 10 minutes
Cook time: 20 minutes
Serves: 12

Tools:

- 12-cup standard muffin pan
- Paper muffin liners (optional)
- Spatula
- 2 medium mixing bowls
- Small bowl
- Wire cooling rack

Ingredients:

- 1 tablespoon ground flaxseed + 3 tablespoons water
- ¾ cup (180 ml) oat milk
- 1 tablespoon apple cider vinegar
- ½ cup (100 g) brown sugar
- ½ cup (125 g) applesauce
- 3 cups (270 g) rolled oats
- 1 teaspoon baking powder
- 1 teaspoon baking soda
- 2 teaspoons ground cinnamon
- ½ teaspoon ground ginger
- ¼ teaspoon ground nutmeg
- 2 medium apples, peeled and cored

Instructions:

1. Preheat your oven to 350F (180C) degrees and line a 12-cup muffin tin with paper liners.
2. In a small bowl, mix the ground flax with the water and set aside for a few minutes until it becomes a gel, also known as a 'flax egg'.
3. In a medium mixing bowl, combine the oat milk with the apple cider vinegar and set aside for 3–4 minutes. The mixture will start to curdle and form a vegan buttermilk.
4. While you're waiting for the vegan buttermilk and flax egg, grate one apple and dice the second one.
5. In a food processor or a high-speed blender, grind 2½ cups (225 g) rolled oats into fine flour.
6. To the bowl with the oat buttermilk, add the brown sugar, applesauce, grated apple, and flax egg. Mix well and set aside.
7. In a separate medium mixing bowl, combine the oat flour, baking powder, baking soda, cinnamon, ginger, and nutmeg.
8. Gently stir the dry ingredients into the wet, just until a smooth batter forms. Using a spatula, fold in the rolled oats and diced apples.
9. Evenly divide the batter between the 12 muffin cups and transfer to the oven. Bake until the muffins turn golden-brown and a toothpick inserted into the center comes out clean, around 18–20 minutes.
10. Leave the muffins to cool for 10 minutes before removing from the muffin tin and serving.

Maya Ross is passionate about the arts, writing, and cooking. She loves to travel and explore cultures. Maya has lived in many countries including the UK, France, and Japan and speaks five languages. She has worked on performing arts productions and festivals in the USA, Cambodia, and France. In October 2019, she will begin her studies at East 15 Acting School in South End, England where she will pursue her BA in World Performance.

CURRIED WINTER SQUASH AND APPLE SOUP

In the Garden of Eden, we can imagine Eve surrounded by fruit and vegetables throughout the seasons. This recipe uses the infamous apple as a key ingredient to create a comforting soup.

Winter squash and apples work beautifully together in this creamy soup. Top with toasted pumpkin seeds or fresh cilantro and serve with bread and an autumn salad.

Prep time: 10 minutes
Cook time: 1 hour
Serves: 6

Tools:

- Baking sheet
- Vegetable peeler
- Parchment paper
- Large soup pot
- Immersion blender or blender

Ingredients:

- 1–2 lbs. (450–900 g) winter squash, peeled, seeded, and cut into ¾-inch diced pieces (my favorite is butternut squash)
- 6 apples, peeled, cored, and cut into ¾-inch pieces
- 1 tablespoon plus 1 teaspoon coconut palm or brown sugar
- ¼ teaspoon sea salt, or to taste
- ½ cup (125 ml) water
- ⅓ cup (30 g) shallots, chopped
- 2 teaspoons Madras curry powder
- ¼ teaspoon ground cardamom
- ¼ teaspoon ground coriander
- 6 cups (250 ml) vegetable broth
- 1 (2 ½-inch) cinnamon stick
- 3 tablespoons chopped fresh cilantro (optional)
- Toasted pumpkin seeds (optional)

Instructions:

1. Preheat your oven to 400°F (220°C) degrees.
2. Line a large baking sheet with a piece of parchment paper and add the chopped squash and apples. Toss with coconut palm sugar, salt, and water.
3. Roast the squash and apples until fork-tender, around 30 minutes, adding small splashes of vegetable broth during roasting, if necessary, to prevent burning.
4. Once done, remove 1 cup apples, cut into small pieces and set aside.
5. In a large soup pot over medium heat add broth, shallots, remaining sugar, curry powder, cardamom, and coriander. Bring to a boil and simmer for 5 minutes or until the shallots are soft.
6. Add squash and apples and blend the soup using a handheld immersion blender or in batches with a conventional blender.
7. Return the soup to the pot and place over medium heat. Add the cinnamon stick and bring the heat to a rapid simmer. Reduce heat to low and let the soup simmer away for 15–20 minutes, stirring occasionally.
8. Taste and adjust the seasoning with more salt and pepper as needed. Discard the cinnamon stick and serve the warm soup garnished with cilantro, pumpkin seeds, and reserved apples.

Andrea Livingston *has been working in the organic food and agriculture sector for almost 20 years. She earned her bachelor's degree in Environmental Studies with an emphasis on Human Health and Sustainable Agriculture from Prescott College in Arizona. Upon graduation, she apprenticed in Ecological Horticulture at the University of California, Santa Cruz and spent ten years managing and operating professional organic farms in California and Washington States. Since 2008 she has worked as a private holistic chef and educator as well as a recipe developer for private clients, health food companies, fitness studios, doctors, and nutrition professionals.*

SARAH

STORY

Sarah is the first Jewish woman and her story is intertwined with that of her husband, Abraham. Originally Sarai and Abram, in old age she and her husband change their names to Sarah and Abraham as a sign of devotion to God.

God asks them to leave their home, promising them a new land and life in Canaan. When they approach Egypt, Abraham fears he will be killed if Sarah's beauty attracts the king's attention. He asks her to pretend to be his sister. The king does attempt to take Sarah as a wife and hearing that she is married to Abraham, releases her.

Having been promised by God that they will create a large nation, Sarah's infertility is a source of confusion and pain. Sarah suggests that Abraham has a child with her handmaid, Hagar. Abraham and Hagar's relationship and Hagar's ability to bear a child, Ishmael, make Sarah jealous and bring tension into their household.

One day, three messengers pass by Sarah and Abraham's tent. Abraham welcomes them with Sarah's help. Sarah has already transitioned through menopause, and when she overhears the messengers tell Abraham that she will have a child, she laughs. Sarah later gives birth to a child and names him Yitzhak, from the hebrew root "to laugh."

When Sarah dies, Abraham pays a large sum for land to bury her. This place is known as *Me'arat Hamachpelah* (Cave of the Patriarchs).

VERSES

"And Abraham and Sarah were old, advanced in years, Sarah no longer had her woman's flow. And Sarah laughed inwardly, saying, "After being shriveled, shall I have the pleasure, and my husband is old?" And the LORD said to Abraham, "Why is it that Sarah laughed, saying, 'Shall I really give birth, old as I am?'"

—Genesis 18: 11–13

"And Abraham was a hundred years old when Isaac his son was born to him. And Sarah said, "Laughter has God made me, Whoever hears will laugh at me."

—Genesis 21: 5–6

THEMES

Adventure

Sarah is constantly on the move. She leaves her home and embarks on a journey. She has to be brave, resourceful, and willing to encounter new things.

Laughter

Sarah's response to the news that she will get pregnant is to laugh. At first she denies that she laughed, but once she gives birth she says "God has brought me laughter."

MIDRASH

Sarah laughed within herself or regarding her inside- she reflected on her physical condition, saying, "is it possible that this womb shall bear a child, that these dried-up breasts will give forth milk?"
—*Midrash Tanchuma, Shoftim* 18

Why does Sarah laugh "*b'kirbah*"? This word can be translated as "to herself" as in "Sarah laughed to herself." Or it can be translated as "about her inside," as in "Sarah laughed about her inside (her body)."

When reading this scene in the Torah, we do not know the tone of Sarah's laughter. Was it embittered, joyous or mocking? Is her laughter a spontaneous reaction to joyous news? Or a grimly mocking response to the mere suggestion of this possibility? This midrash, however, imagines Sarah laughing darkly at the idea that her body is still fertile in her old age.

In a biblical society where women's central role was to produce children, we can imagine that Sarah laughed bitterly at the contradiction that her aged body would be fertile when her youth had given her persistent and enduring infertility. Her mocking of her body is both sad and familiar. Thousands of years have passed and laughter still provides us with relief from the intense emotions, whether negative or positive, that we attach to our bodies.

As we continue to interpret these verses over time, perhaps we can read Sarah's laughter as defiant or joyous instead of self-loathing. The story illustrates that there are many ways to laugh. We can laugh mockingly or cruelly at ourselves. We can also use laughter as an effective tool to lighten our days and navigate the changes in our bodies, and to cherish both the changes and our laughter as gifts from God.

PROMPTS

What role does laughter play in your life? In your spiritual life?

What do you consider to be your life adventures? What have you learned from them?

What are the changes in your body that you have found challenging? If you could learn to laugh at them, what would that give you?

Rena Singer *is a rabbinical student at Hebrew Union College – Jewish Institute of Religion in New York. Rena is the co-founder of the Instagram and online community called Modern Ritual. Rena will receive rabbinic ordination in 2020.*

KALE WITH HORSERADISH HEMP SEED DRESSING AND POPPED AMARANTH

Sarah is reported to have been a "master of deeds and kindness" and her name means "princess." I imagine that she was a lovely hostess – one who would serve this show-stopping, colorful, flavorful dish. While there are a few different tasks involved in this recipe, it is well worth the extra effort to delight your guests (and yourself!) as Sarah would have done.

The health benefits come from kale, one of the most nutrient-dense foods, and almonds which provide fiber and boost your heart health. Hemp hearts are a complete protein and a balanced source of Omega 3 and Omega 6 essential fatty-acids. If you'd like to make this dish heartier, toss in lentils or chickpeas.

Prep time: 10 minutes

Cook time: 10 minutes

Serves: 4–6

Tools:

- Large saucepan
- Splatter guard
- Small bowl
- Small sauce pot
- Chef's knife
- Cutting board
- Large mixing bowl
- Measuring spoons and cups
- Blender

Ingredients:

- ½ cup (45 g) raw amaranth
- 1 bunch kale, destemmed and roughly chopped or torn
- 3–4 dried unsweetened, unsulfured apricots
- ¼ cup (20 g) hemp hearts
- 1 2-inch piece horseradish, peeled and roughly chopped
- 1 tablespoon lemon juice
- 4 small fresh apricots, sliced into thin wedges (alternatively, roughly chop 8–10 dried apricots)
- 1 shallot, peeled and minced
- 1 large handful flat leaf parsley, roughly chopped
- ½ cup (65 g) roughly chopped toasted almonds
- Salt and pepper to taste

Instructions:

1. Place a medium bowl next to the stove.
2. Heat a tall pot on the stove over high heat. The surface should be really hot so that the amaranth pops and does not burn. Pour a drop of water into the pot. When the water evaporates immediately upon contact, add 2 tablespoons of the amaranth.
3. Use the splatter guard as a shield to prevent the popped amaranth from flying out of the pot, but do not cover the pot with the lid or the heat will be trapped and the amaranth will burn.
4. Transfer the amaranth to the bowl once it has popped and becomes white, like baby popcorn. Repeat this process until all of the amaranth is popped. You should have about 1 cup. Note that sometimes the first batch acts similarly to the first pancake. If it burns and you need to throw it out, there will still be enough.
5. To make the dressing, soak the dried apricots in recently boiled water for about 10 minutes.
6. Transfer the apricots into a blender and add in ½ cup of water, hemp hearts, horseradish, and lemon juice. Blend until smooth and season with salt and pepper to taste. Place in the fridge to chill for a few minutes.
7. To assemble, place the kale in a large bowl and use your hands to massage in enough dressing so that the leaves are evenly coated. You may have leftover dressing depending on the size of the bunch of kale – it will last in the fridge for up to a week. Season with salt and pepper to taste.
8. Fold in the minced shallot, most of the parsley, most of the fresh apricot slices or chopped dried apricots and most of the almonds, setting aside some of each to garnish.
9. To serve, top with amaranth and remaining parsley, apricots, and almonds.

Lauren Chandler *has been teaching whole food seasonal cooking classes for more than twenty years. Lauren is based in Portland, Oregon, USA. She runs her own business, where she offers recipe and menu development, chef services and supports individuals with all food preferences in reaching their cooking and dietary goals.*

CHOCOLATE ZUCCHINI CAKE

The story of Sarah makes me think about how women deal with strong emotion. Sometimes we act badly towards others, sometimes we treat ourselves badly, or both. When Sarah was experiencing sadness about not having her own child and overcome with jealousy towards Hagar for being able to have a child so easily and quickly, what did she eat?

Sometimes when we feel sad or angry, we punish ourselves by eating too little, too much or by consuming foods that are not good for us. I offer this healthy chocolate cake as a nourishing treat for Sarah.

This dairy and oil free cake is moist, tender and full of flavor from the nutritious addition of zucchini. It gets better as it sits out as the zucchini will keep the cake moist and scrumptious. It is the perfect addition to your afternoon cup of coffee or tea.

Prep time: 10 minutes
Cook time: 40 minutes
Serves: 4–6

Tools:

- Large mixing bowl
- Whisk
- Medium mixing bowl
- 8×8 baking dish
- Wire cooling rack
- Spatula

Ingredients:

- 1 cup (130 g) all-purpose flour/ gluten-free all-purpose flour
- ⅓ cup (30 g) unsweetened cocoa powder
- ¾ cup (180 g) raw sugar
- 1 teaspoon baking powder
- ½ teaspoon baking soda
- ½ teaspoon sea salt
- ½ teaspoon cinnamon
- 1 cup (150 g) zucchini, finely grated
- ¼ cup (60 ml) non-dairy milk
- ½ cup (125 g) applesauce
- 1 teaspoon pure vanilla extract
- Confectioners sugar, for dusting
- Fresh berries, to serve

Instructions:

1. Preheat your oven to 350°F (180°C) degrees.
2. In a large mixing bowl, sift together the flour, cocoa powder, sugar, baking soda, baking powder, salt, and cinnamon.
3. In a separate mixing bowl, stir together the zucchini, milk, applesauce, and vanilla extract.
4. Transfer the wet ingredients into the dry and fold the two together until well-combined, taking care not to overmix the batter.
5. Lightly oil a baking dish and pour in the batter. Smooth the top with a spatula.
6. Bake for 40 minutes, or until a toothpick inserted in the center comes out clean.
7. Remove cake from oven and allow to cool for 10 minutes before removing from the cake pan and allow to cool completely on a wire cooling rack.
8. Serve garnished with confectioners sugar and fresh berries.

From the Jewish Food Hero Kitchen

HAGAR

STORY

Hagar is an Egyptian woman who serves in Abraham and Sarah's household as Sarah's servant. When Sarah is unable to conceive a child, she instructs Abraham to conceive a son with Hagar, so that he will be able to fulfill God's promise of having many children. Yet when Hagar becomes pregnant, Sarah mistreats her. Hagar attempts to escape, but an angel of God appears to her and instructs her to return, telling her that her son will be wild, and will be called Ishmael. Before returning, Hagar says, "You are a God who Sees (*El Ro'i*),…for even here, haven't I seen the God who sees me?" (Gen 16:13). Hagar returns and gives birth to a son, Ishmael.

When Sarah's son Isaac is weaned, she mistreats Hagar once again, this time banishing her and Ishmael to the wilderness, where Hagar loses hope. She sets her son down under a bush, and not wishing to witness his death, she walks away. Hagar begins to cry, saying: "Let me not look upon the death of the child." An angel answers, showing her a well and saving them from dying of thirst. With God's protection, Hagar and Ishmael survive and prosper.

VERSES

"And he said, "Hagar, slavegirl of Sarai! Where have you come from and where are you going?" And she said, "From Sarai my mistress I am fleeing."

—Genesis 16:8

"And when the water in the skin was gone, she flung the child under one of the bushes and went off and sat down at a distance, a bowshot away, for she thought, "Let me not see when the child dies." And she sat at a distance and raised her voice and wept. And God heard the voice of the lad and God's messenger called out from the heavens and said to her, "What troubles you. Hagar? Fear not, for God has heard the lad's voice where he is."

—Genesis 21:16–17

"And God opened her eyes and she saw a well of water, and she went and filled the skin with water and gave to the lad to drink."

—Genesis 21:19

THEMES

Finding Your Own Voice

Within her own household, Hagar has little power. No words of conversation between her and Sarah or between her and Abraham are recorded in the Biblical text. Yet when the stakes are raised, she finds her voice and confides in an angel of God.

Resilience

Hagar survives mistreatment not once but twice. An angel of God speaks to Hagar on both occasions that she leaves the household, and she is willing to hear a new perspective. When she is despondent at the idea of losing her son, she hears the angel of God speaking to her. Her ability to hear and speak to the angel allows her and Ishmael to survive in a harsh environment.

MIDRASH

"Hagar would tell them: 'My mistress Sarai is not inwardly what she is outwardly: she appears to be a righteous woman, but she is not. For had she been a righteous woman, see how many years have passed without her conceiving, whereas I conceived in one night!'"

—*Bereishit Rabbah* 45:4

This midrash explores two elements of the tense relationship between two women in an impossible situation and points to two common human failings: behaving badly in intimate relationships and viewing a woman's fertility as representative of her character.

Hagar's claims of Sarah's abusive behaviour might not be believed. It is hard to accept that Sarah might have behaved so badly to anyone. No matter how well Sarah is perceived by others, how Hagar feels treated by Sarah is also important. It can be difficult to consider that someone we respect or revere may have treated others poorly. Particularly when the victim, in this case, Hagar, does not have power, we do well to listen to them and consider their story. Often a victim has much more to lose than to gain by speaking up, and we owe them the dignity of listening to their story.

Hagar's story reminds us that we may not like accepting that those who we respect are fallible, but this is a part of developing our own character and defining the rules of the society in which we hope to live.

Hagar's story illustrates that we all have the capacity to behave badly, and indeed we all have to guard against behaving badly with certain people, perhaps particularly with those close to us and in family relationships.

Hagar's view of fertility – her own and Sarah's – is deeply and mystically connected to character, thoughts and actions. Both Hagar and the Rabbis try to make sense of the imbalance in fertility between Hagar and Sarah. Why was Hagar able to conceive so easily whereas Sarah struggled to become pregnant most of her life? Was the treatment Hagar received from Sarah justified as the balancing force to Sarah's fortune in fertility? Earlier in the text, the midrash suggests that righteous women never conceive during the first act of intercourse. Such a suggestion would justify the harsh treatment Hagar receives from Sarah as the natural consequence for falling pregnant immediately – the physical sign of unrighteousness.

While today we know that fertility has nothing to do with character, we might still be foolishly tempted to perceive a causal relationship between a woman's moral conduct and her physical health.

Most Midrashim show Sarah in a more positive light as she is a matriarch of our tradition. Although this is comforting, it is not the whole story. Perhaps what we can learn most from Hagar's story is that the surface story is true but it is not the truth. To have a more complete understanding about any relationship conflict or personal experience with fertility, we must be the person experiencing it. We must also accept that no two experiences with conflict or fertility are the same. Perhaps it is our role to notice our own assumptions, judgments, and biases and ask others about their experiences before jumping in.

PROMPTS

What are some of the societal factors that play into your characterization of Hagar and Sarah in this story?

When have there been opportunities for you to judge someone harshly, or kindly? What contributed to your thought process?

How might we make room in our hearts to respond with openness to someone who is in pain – even when we are in pain ourselves?

Samantha Frank is a Rabbi in the United States. Originally from Silver Spring, MD, she has served as Rabbinic Intern at the Slifka Center for Jewish Life at Yale, Temple Beth Am in Monessen, PA, and most recently, Temple Micah in Washington, DC. She co-creates Modern Ritual, an Instagram account that models passionate, resonant Jewish life. She will receive her Rabbinic Ordination from Hebrew Union College-Jewish Institute of Religion in 2019 and lives in New York, NY. One of three sisters, she loves family and macaroni and cheese.

BLENDED CUCUMBER, AVOCADO, AND MINT SOUP

On a purely physical level, the story of Hagar shows a woman and her son overheated, thirsty, and dehydrated. This recipe attends to her body first and seeks to offer her immediate coolness and hydration. The cucumber is a cooling fruit filled with essential water.

This creamy cucumber and avocado soup is the perfect refreshing meal for a warm summer day. The cucumber is packed with essential nutrients and water, while the avocado brings in a good dose of heart-healthy fats. Don't skip the mint though – it adds a bright taste and a bit of zing to the soup.

Prep time: 10 minutes
Cook time: assembly only
Serves: 4–6

Tools:

- Blender
- Knife

Ingredients:

- 2 avocados, pitted and halved
- 6 small persian cucumbers, washed and roughly chopped
- One bunch of mint
- ¼ cup (60 ml) oat milk
  ½ lemon, juiced
- Salt and pepper to taste

Instructions:

1. Scoop the avocado flesh straight into a high-speed blender and add in the chopped cucumbers. Add in the mint and the oat milk and blend on the highest setting possible until a smooth and creamy soup forms, around 30–40 seconds.
2. Season the soup with a fat pinch of salt and pepper and transfer into the fridge to chill for a minimum of 2 hours.
3. Once the soup is chilled, stir in the lemon juice and spoon into bowls. Garnish with chopped almonds, pumpkin seeds, or chia seeds.

Helene Abiola is a former Division one athlete with a lifelong passion for health and wellness. She has a Masters degree in Community Health Education and her public health work allows her to make NYC a healthier place for the nearly 400,000 employees in her agency. Helene lives in NYC with her son Harvey. Whenever there's free time you can catch her exploring the many restaurants, parks, and cultural sites across the city.

ROSE AND HONEY HALVAH

Hagar walked away from Abraham and Sarah's home without sufficient food for herself and her son. Perhaps she did not have time to prepare for her family's journey or was not given adequate provisions by Abraham and Sarah. Either way, she ends up in a dangerous situation alone in the desert with her son without food and water. Halvah would have been a good choice for Hagar as it is compact food that gives energy and minerals.

Halvah is a multicultural sweet confection present in Jewish and Arab cuisines. This type of halvah has a crumbly texture as it is made from tahini (sesame seed paste). It can be stored for a good while in the fridge, so it is a great option to make ahead of time and keep on hand for when guests come over.

Prep time: 10 minutes
Cook time: 15 minutes
Serves: 8–10

Tools:

- 2 small pots
- Candy thermometer
- Measuring cups and spoons
- Wooden spoon
- Loaf pan
- Parchment paper

Ingredients:

- 1 cup (320 g) honey
- ¾ cup (170 g) smooth tahini
- ½ cup (55 g) slivered almonds, toasted (optional)
- 2 teaspoons rose water (optional – you can replace with a teaspoon of vanilla extract or a ¼ teaspoon of almond extract)

Instructions:

1. Add the honey to a small pot with a candy thermometer attached and place over medium heat. Heat until the thermometer reaches 240F (115C) degrees.

2. While the honey is coming up to temperature, give the tahini a good stir making sure it's even and no oil is separating, then set it aside in the second small pot.

3. Once the honey reaches temperature, set it aside and clean the candy thermometer.

4. Place the candy thermometer into the pot with the tahini and place over medium heat. Heat the tahini until it reaches 120F (50C) degrees.

5. Pour the warmed tahini into the honey and mix well with a wooden spoon until the mixture becomes really smooth and shiny. It may take a few minutes, but eventually the mixture will come together nicely.

6. Stir in the rose water and the nuts, if using, and continue stirring until it becomes fairly stiff, around 5–7 minutes.

7. Pour the mixture into a loaf pan lined with parchment paper. Set it aside to cool to room temperature, then transfer into the fridge for 24–36 hours. This will allow the halvah to form sugar crystals and reach the desired crumbly texture.

8. Slice with a sharp knife and store any leftovers in the fridge.

From the Jewish Food Hero Kitchen

REBEKAH

STORY

Rebekah (Rivka), second of the matriarchs, was born in Ur Kasdim, Abraham's birthplace. Rivkah's father is Bethuel, making her Abraham's great niece, and her brother is Lavan. Avraham sends his servant Eliezer to Ur Kasdim to find a wife for Avraham's son, Yitzhak. When Eliezer arrives, he waits beside the wells and prays to Hashem to send him a woman who will offer to water his camels as a sign that she will make a good wife for Yitzhak. At that moment, Rivkah emerges, and when Eliezer asks her for water, she draws water not only for him, but also for his camels. Rivkah's family hosts Eliezer that night, and Betuel and Lavan agree that Rivkah can marry Yitzhak. They ask for her to stay with them for ten months or a year before she leaves, but Rivkah convinces them to allow her to go immediately. Rivkah and Eliezer return to Avraham's house, and when Rivkah sees Yitzhak for the first time, she falls off her camel and asks Eliezer who he is. When Eliezer tells Rivkah that the man is Yitzhak, her future husband, she covers her face with her veil.

Yitzhak and Rivkah get married, but Rivkah is barren for many years. Yitzhak prays for children opposite Rivkah, and she becomes pregnant. Rivkah, feeling her children struggling within her, asks Hashem why this is happening to her, and he replies that there are two nations in her womb, and the older child will grow to serve the younger one. Rivkah gives birth to twins, birthing Eisav first, followed by Yaakov.

Years later, Yitzhak is growing old and is ready to give Eisav the bechora, the blessing for the oldest son. Rivkah, overhearing Yitzhak's conversation with Eisav, decides that Yaakov should have the bracha instead and springs into action. She prepares meat for Yaakov to bring to Yitzhak, dresses Yaakov in skins so that he feels hairy like Eisav, and sends him to get the bracha instead of his brother. Yitzhak is tricked into giving Yaakov the bracha, but when Eisav hears what happened, he wants to kill Yaakov, so Rivkah sends him away to Lavan to protect him. The last time Rivkah appears in the Torah, she tells Yitzhak that she is fed up with her life because of the daughters of Chet, and asks what her purpose would be if Yaakov married one of them.

VERSES

"And she said, "Drink my lord," and she hurried and lowered her jug onto her hand and let him drink. And she let him drink his fill and said, "For your camels, too, I shall draw water until they drink their fill." And she hurried and emptied her jug into the well to draw water and drew water for all his camels."

—Genesis 24:18–20

"And Rebekah raised her eyes and saw Isaac, and she alighted from the camel. And she said to the servant, "Who is that man walking through the field toward us?" And the servant said, "He is my master," and she took her veil and covered her face.

—Genesis 24:64–65

"And the children clashed together within her, and she said, "Then why me?" and she went to inquire of the LORD. And the LORD said to her:
"Two nations – in your womb,
two people from your loins shall issue.
People over people shall prevail,
the elder, the younger's slave."

—Genesis 25:22–24

THEMES

Selflessness

Rivkah was always focused on the needs of others rather than herself. When Eliezer, a stranger, showed up in Ur Kasdim and asked for water, Rivkah drew water for him and his camels until they were all sated. Eliezer brought ten camels, so Rivkah clearly drew copious amounts of water. However, the Torah emphasizes that Rivkah *rushed* to draw the water for Eliezer and his camels despite the enormity of the task. Later, Eliezer asks Rivkah to return with him right away to marry Yitzhak, but Betuel and Lavan want Rivkah to stay with them for another year before she leaves. Rivkah assents to leaving at once, putting the needs of Eliezer, Yitzhak and Avraham before her own.

Empowerment

Rivkah is an extremely active character, never waiting around for other people to do things for her. When she feels her children fighting in her stomach, rather than ignore it or wait for it to cease on its own, she decides to go to Hashem and find out why this is happening. Once Rivkah finds out that

Yitzhak is ready to give Eisav the bechora, she immediately takes charge and does what is required so that Yaakov can receive the bracha instead of Eisav. She is an active player in her own life, never content to wait for others to do what must be done.

MIDRASH

"Rabbi Yitzhak says: If this is to teach us that Rivkah is from Aram Naharaim, doesn't it already say 'from Paddan Aram'? What is the purpose of stating that Rivkah is 'an Aramean,' 'the daughter of an Aramean,' and 'the brothers of Lavan the Aramean'? Rather, this comes to teach us that her father was sly and her brother was sly, and even the people of the land were sly, but Rikvah emerged from them a tzadeket, like a rose among thorns."

—Genesis *Rabbah* 63:4

When Rivkah and Yitzhak get married, the Torah unnecessarily repeats that Rivkah is the daughter of Betuel and the sister of Lavan. The midrash explains that this repetition is to emphasize that Rivkah is like a "lily among thorns," still a tzadeket, a righteous woman, even though she grew up among wicked people. This emphasizes how impressive it is that Rivkah is a good person despite the family amongst whom she grew up. (*Bereshit Rabbah* 63:4) Because of this, miracles happened for Rivkah. When Eliezer first sees Rivkah as she goes to draw water for her family, the midrash explains that all the other women drew water up from the well toward them, but for Rivkah, the water came up to meet her on its own. Hashem said that just as the water ascended for Rivkah, so too the water ascended to meet Bnei Yisrael (the Israelites) from their well in Arnon in the desert (on their journey from Egypt to the Land of Israel). (*Bereshit Rabbah* 60:5) Based on this midrash, Rivkah was a person to whom even inanimate objects were drawn. Furthermore, in her merit, an entire nation was provided with water and life.

PROMPTS

We are all so busy caring for our friends and family and those in our "inner" circle. How do we think about the 'other' in our midst; the stranger or the lonely? Do we make them a part of our communities? What do we do for them?

Do I rush to help a person or a community, or do I drag myself to what I perceive as a social 'requirement'?

Much of the Rivkah story centers around communication – between mothers and sons, and husbands and wives. What would I do if I sensed that someone close to me was making a misinformed or weak decision? Would I intervene? Is it possible to do so while also protecting the relationship?

Josephine Schizer is a junior at the Ramaz Upper School in Manhattan. An avid writer, she is a member of the Fresh Ink for Teens editorial board and writes for her school newspaper. Additionally, she co-founded Ramaz's engineering club; is a member of the Ramaz Model Congress, Science Olympiad, and Varsity Tennis teams; and spends time with Holocaust survivors in the Witness Theater program. Outside of school, she organizes a monthly women's tefillah group at her synagogue, Congregation Ramath Orah, and is a member of Food Allergy Research and Education (FARE)'s Teen Advisory Group.

LENTIL AND TOMATO STEW WITH TAMARIND

Rebekah's story is forever tied to lentils. This lentil stew includes a special ingredient: tamarind paste. It gives the stew the sour element that perfectly balances all the flavors. When looking at Rebekah's story, it is clear that this nuclear family never found their balance point.

Although you can make this stew on your stovetop, it is more delicious in the pressure cooker because this method of cooking intensifies the flavors. You can use different vegetables based on what's in season or what you have lying around – zucchini, leeks, broccoli, and cauliflower will all work.

Prep time: 10 minutes
Cook time: 45 minutes
Serves: 6–8

Tools:

- Large stew pot or pressure cooker
- Prep bowl
- Good knife
- Colander

Ingredients:

- 1 cup red lentils
- ½ cup green lentils
- 1 15.5-oz. (450 g) can of kidney beans, rinsed and drained
- 4 ½ cups water (or vegetable broth)
- 2 onions, diced
- 2 red peppers, diced
- 2 shallots, diced
- 4 cloves garlic, minced
- 6 medium tomatoes, diced
- 4 tablespoons tomato paste
- 1 ½ teaspoon chili powder (add more to increase the heat)
- 3 teaspoons ground cumin
- 2 teaspoons salt
- 1 teaspoon cinnamon
- 1 tablespoon tamarind paste
- 2 teaspoons light brown sugar

Instructions:

1. Add onions, garlic, and shallots to a stew pot and pour in ¼ cup of water. Place over medium heat and cook, stirring occasionally, until the onion is translucent, around 5–7 minutes.

2. Stir in the chopped tomatoes, red pepper, and tomato paste; continue simmering over medium heat.

3. Add in the cumin, chili, tamarind paste, and brown sugar; stir to coat all the vegetables with the spices.

4. Add the red and green lentils and pour in the water. Bring the soup to a boil, then lower the heat to medium-low, and let the soup simmer away for 25 minutes or until the lentils are cooked.

5. Once the lentils are cooked, stir in the canned kidney beans and season with 2 teaspoons of salt.

6. Remove the stew from the heat and allow to sit, covered, for another 10 minutes. Taste and add more salt or spices, if necessary.

7. To make the stew using the pressure cooker, follow the same instructions up to step 4 and pressure-cook the lentils for 5 minutes.

8. Serve warm stew over a whole grain or with a baked potato.

From the Jewish Food Hero Kitchen

RASPBERRY LEMON MELTAWAYS

In Rebekah's story, we see her sons battling one another in a fight for power. The difficult family dynamics are sour, just like the taste of the lemon. This was the inspiration behind my raw lemon raspberry meltaways.

The recipe contains lemon peel, a natural source of vitamin C and calcium. Usually filled with butter and coated in sugar, meltaways are not a particularly healthy dessert. I've created a healthier meltaway cookie version with shredded coconut and freeze-dried raspberries.

Prep time: 10 minutes
Cook time: assembly only
Serves: 12

Tools

- Medium food processor
- Small bowl
- Spatula
- Measuring cups and spoons or a scale

Ingredients:

- ¾ cup (105 g) freeze-dried raspberries, divided into two
- 1 cup (100 g) shredded coconut
- 1 ½ cups (144 g) almond flour
- ¼ cup (57 g) lemon juice (about two lemons)
- ¼ cup (85 g) agave
- ⅓ cup (43 g) coconut flour
- 1 tablespoon lemon zest (about one lemon)
- ½ teaspoon salt

Instructions:

1. In a food processor, process ½ cup (70 g) of freeze-dried raspberries into a fine powder. Set aside.

2. Place the shredded coconut in a food processor and blend for 2 minutes. Add in the almond flour, coconut flour, agave, lemon juice, lemon zest, and salt; continue blending until a dough forms, another minute or two.

3. Stir in the remaining ¼ cup (35 g) of freeze-dried raspberries.

4. Using a cookie scoop or wet hands, roll the dough into a dozen balls and coat each ball in raspberry powder.

5. Serve chilled and enjoy! The cookies can be refrigerated for up to a week.

Jacqueline Landy is in eighth grade at the Ramaz Middle School in Manhattan. She adores all elements of the culinary world. This led her to create Baked By Jax, a dessert blog and Instagram account. She co-founded the bi-monthly challah bake at school, which successfully sells out of loaves each sale.

RACHEL

STORY

Rachel is one of the matriarchs of the Jewish people. Her father is Laban, the brother of Rebekah, and she has a sister named Leah. Rachel works as a shepherd and her name means "ewe," which connects her deeply to the animals that she tends.

Rachel is known in the Torah for her beauty. Her future husband Jacob is captivated by the sight of her when he first sees her at the well watering her flock. Jacob is intent on marrying Rachel and Laban convinces him to work in his household for seven years to earn his daughter. Jacob fulfills this promise, but on the wedding night Laban switches Rachel for Leah. Jacob unknowingly marries the wrong woman, and must work an additional seven years to marry Rachel.

The jealousy and competition between the sisters who share a husband is exacerbated when Rachel struggles to bear children. Meanwhile, Leah, Leah's maidservant Zilpah, and Rachel's maidservant Bilhah, collectively have 10 sons with Jacob. Rachel finally gives birth to a son, Joseph. Eventually Jacob leaves Laban's house with his wives, concubines, and their children. On the way out, Rachel grabs Laban's idols. Rachel dies giving birth to her second son, Benjamin, and is buried in Bethlehem.

VERSES

"And Rachel saw that she had born no children to Jacob, and Rachel was jealous of her sister, and she said to Jacob, Give me sons, for if you don't, I am a dead woman!"

—Genesis 30:1

"And God remembered Rachel and God heard her and he opened her womb…"

—Genesis 30:22

"And it happened, when she was laboring hardest in the birth, that the midwife said to her, "Fear not, for this one, too, is a son for you.""

—Genesis 35:17

THEMES

Patience

Rachel exercises patience when her father Laban arranges a swap with her sister and she has to wait seven more years to marry Jacob. She deeply wants to become a mother, and painfully endures years of infertility until her first son Joseph is born. Patience does not mean acceptance, and Rachel is quite expressive of her discontent throughout the biblical narrative. Still, she never loses sight of her goal and immediately after Joseph's birth, she expresses optimism that God will once again bless her with a child in the future.

Action

The corollary to her enduring patience is her ability to take decisive action at the correct moments. After waiting years to become pregnant with no success, Rachel tells Jacob to take her maidservant Bilhah as a wife. Bilhah has two sons who Rachel adopts. When Reuben brings his mother Leah mandrakes, Rachel quickly negotiates with Leah to give her the mandrakes, at that time believed to be a fertility enhancer. In exchange, she promises to send Jacob to Leah's bed for the night. When Jacob flees from Laban with his wives, children and flocks of animals, Rachel grabs Laban's precious idols. When Laban comes to find them, she sits on them and tells him that she is menstruating so that he won't come any closer. We aren't told of her motive, but rabbis have debated two possibilities for why she took the idols. One is that she took them to wean Laban from idolatry. Alternatively, as idols were used for divination, Rachel took them to keep Laban from consulting them to locate the escaping family. Throughout her life, Rachel's actions are strategic, pragmatic, and show that she is willing to travel an unconventional route to achieve her goals.

MIDRASH

"So Jacob gave her certain distinguishing signs that she should use to indicate to him that she was actually Rachel and not her sister. When the wedding night arrived, and Laban planned to switch the sisters, Rachel said to herself: Now my sister will be embarrassed, for Jacob will ask her for the signs and she will not know them. So she gave them to her."

—Babylonian Talmud *Megillah* 13b

Relationships between women, whether sisters or friends, have immense power. Rachel and Leah struggle in their relationship, and the narrative of their story weaves together moments of great animosity with times of coming together, when they speak literally in one voice. Rachel was capable of compassion for her less-beautiful sister Leah, the one who Jacob married by accident but never desired. But compassion alone was not enough to keep her from resenting Leah's effortless fertility and lashing out at her. Leah was bitterly envious of Rachel's beauty and Jacob's admiration and love of her. These sisters were placed in an impossible situation of having to share a husband. It was this context that gave rise to their extreme emotions. However, the emotions triggered in their undeniably loaded situation are common to relationships. How might their relationship have been different if they could have comforted one another in their insecurities, rather than using these weaknesses as targets for attack? Their story instructs us to be generous with our support of our sisters and friends, and to be sensitive towards their perceived weaknesses. In the safety of these bonds we can find comfort and support, and it is upon us to be both gracious and vulnerable.

PROMPTS

What have you wanted so badly that you felt you would die if you did not receive it?

What is the closest female relationship in your life? What brings you close to this person? What pulls you apart?

How do you balance patience and action in your life? Which tendency is stronger for you?

Rachel uses the taboo of menstruation to deceive her father. Does a person deserve to be deceived by way of their own prejudice? Why or why not?

Rabbi Sara Rich is the Executive Director of the Hillel of Buffalo, which facilitates Jewish experiences, community-building and leadership development for undergraduate and graduate students in the Buffalo area. She was raised in Maryland, studied in Jerusalem at the Pardes Institute of Jewish Studies, and was ordained as a rabbi in 2011 from the Hebrew Union College-Jewish Institute of Religion in New York. She is a mother, a wife, and a home cook always in search of a new recipe. Writing about Rachel for this cookbook was an honor because she has many special Rachels in her life, including her sister and many dear friends.

TOASTED ALMOND BROWN RICE
SALAD WITH DRIED CHERRIES

In Rachel's situation, it could be tempting to use food for comfort.

What we eat has an enormous influence on how we feel. If we over-consume refined sugars, caffeine, alcohol and processed foods, we feel it. Conversely, if the majority of our diet is centred on eating a satiating amount of minimally processed foods, whole grains, vegetables and fruits and drinking plenty of water, it helps us keep grounded.

This brown rice salad is nutty and fresh. The rice and fresh vegetables paired with the tart dried cherries and toasted almonds give the salad an earthy and unexpected flavor. Feel free to substitute quinoa for the brown rice.

Prep time: 10 minutes
Cook time: 45 minutes
Serves: 6–8

Tools:

- Rice cooker/Soup pot with a lid
- Good knife
- Blender
- Salad bowl

Ingredients:

- 3 cups (540 g) medium or long grain brown rice (for 6 cups cooked)
- 2 yellow peppers, diced
- 4 medium tomatoes, seeded and diced
- 1 ¼ cups (125 g) whole almonds, sliced
- 3 long celery stalks, sliced thin
- 1 cup (30 g) sliced spinach
- 4 garlic cloves, minced
- 2 shallots, diced
- ¼ cup (40 g) dried cherries, halved
- ¼ cup (25 g) green onion tops, sliced (the green part only)

For the dressing:
- ½ cup (125 ml) fresh lemon juice
- 2 tablespoons maple syrup or agave
- 1 teaspoon salt, or to taste
- black pepper, to taste

Instructions:

1. Rinse the brown rice under cold water and cook in a rice cooker or on the stove, according to package directions.

2. After the rice is cooked, allow to cool for 5 minutes and then spread it out on a baking sheet and allow to cool for 1 hour. This will keep it from becoming mushy or gummy.

3. Place all diced vegetables, except the spinach, into a salad bowl and set aside.

4. Toast the almonds in a dry skillet until they start to smell nutty and turn a golden color, around 5 minutes. Set aside to cool.

5. Whisk all ingredients for the dressing in a small jar and pour over the vegetables. Give everything a good stir, so all the vegetables are coated with the dressing.

6. Add the rice, spinach, dried cherries, and almonds and mix gently. Taste and adjust the seasoning with more salt or agave, if necessary.

7. Garnish with green onion tops and serve at room temperature or chilled from the fridge.

From the Jewish Food Hero Kitchen

BLOOD ORANGE AND BLACK SESAME POLENTA CAKE

Rachel's story is one of waiting. She waits for fourteen years to marry Jacob, and then she spends years waiting to become a mother before finally giving birth to Joseph. Baking a cake seems particularly fitting for Rachel's narrative: all baking requires patience and faith that the alchemy of ingredients will do their work in the oven while you wait. This recipe is an upside down cake with its beauty only revealed after it is fully baked, unmolded, and flipped over. The wait is rewarded and the resulting cake is sunny and colorful, with a glistening top of rich-colored orange slices that cover the polenta and sesame cake beneath.

This plant-based cake is a healthier take on dessert. Its main source of fat is coconut milk, and it has fiber and protein from the polenta and sesame seeds. While not sugar free, this cake uses it sparingly, and the result is a baked good that isn't too sweet, but is still full of flavor.

Prep time: 10 minutes
Cook time: 45 minutes
Serves: 10–12

Tools:

- 8" or 9" springform cake pan (20–22cm)
- Whisk
- Parchment paper
- Small saucepan
- Microplane/zester
- Large mixing bowl
- Spatula or wooden spoon
- Chopping board
- Knife
- Measuring spoons
- Measuring cups
- Plate/platter

Ingredients:

- 2 blood oranges
- ⅓ cup + ½ cup (130 g) sugar, divided
- 3 tablespoons water
- 1 cup (180 g) fine polenta/cornmeal
- 1 cup (130 g) all-purpose unbleached flour
- 2 teaspoons baking powder
- 1 teaspoon baking soda
- ½ teaspoon kosher salt
- 1 13.6 oz/400 ml can full-fat coconut milk (1 ½ cups)
- 2 tablespoons coconut oil, melted
- 1 tablespoon black sesame seeds, plus more for sprinkling

Instructions:

1. Preheat your oven to 350°F (180°C) degrees.
2. Grease the springform pan with a bit of coconut oil and line the bottom of the pan with parchment paper. Grease the parchment paper as well.
3. Zest one of the blood oranges and reserve the zest. Peel the blood oranges and slice into ½-inch rounds. Evenly layer the blood orange slices on the bottom on the springform pan and sprinkle some black sesame seeds on top.
4. In a small saucepan, combine ⅓ cup of sugar with 3 tablespoons of water. Bring the mixture to a simmer over medium heat, and simmer until the sugar is dissolved, about 3 minutes. Pour the sugar mixture evenly over the orange slices in the cake pan.
5. In a large mixing bowl, whisk together the polenta, flour, ½ a cup of sugar, baking powder, baking soda, and salt.
6. Make a well in the center of the dry ingredients, and add the coconut milk and melted coconut oil. Using a spatula or a wooden spoon, stir together the wet and dry ingredients until just combined; be careful not to overmix. Add the black sesame seeds and reserved blood orange zest and mix until just incorporated.
7. Pour the batter over the sliced blood oranges. Smooth out the batter with the spatula or back of a spoon.
8. Bake until a toothpick inserted into the center of the cake comes out clean, around 45 minutes. Allow the cake to cool in the pan for 20 minutes, then unmold and flip the cake onto a plate/platter so that the bottom with the oranges is now facing up.
9. Allow to fully cool, then slice and serve.

Sonya Sanford is a food writer and avid cook based out of Portland, Oregon, USA. She specializes in Jewish food from around the world, and cooking with seasonal and local ingredients from the farmers' markets where she lives. Her culinary background includes food styling for various media, working as a recipe tester and developer for cookbooks, acting as the chef of successful pop-ups, and teaching cooking classes privately and for large groups. She began her culinary career working as a personal chef in Hollywood.

LEAH

STORY

Leah was the older of two daughters of Lavan and cousin to Jacob. Though Leah was a woman of "tender eyes," Jacob fell in love with her younger sister, Rachel, who was attractive "in body shape and appearance." Lavan gave both daughters to Jacob in marriage, but Jacob loved only Rachel.

In compensation, God made Leah fertile, and she soon gave birth to six sons – Reuven, Shimon, Levi, Judah, Issachar, and Zevulun – and a daughter, Dinah. Thus, Leah quickly became the envy of her younger sister, who was unable to bear children until later years. Eventually, when Jacob's family was complete and he had amassed wealth, Jacob consulted with Leah and Rachel about the prospect of leaving their father's home, secretly, and returning with Jacob to his native Canaan. They agreed, recognising that they had nothing to gain by staying, and they departed by camelback. Upon catching up with the family, Lavan eventually agreed to let them proceed on their way, kissing his daughters farewell and making Jacob vow never to mistreat them.

As the caravan journeyed onward, Jacob anticipated a dangerous encounter with his estranged brother, Esau. He split Leah and her sister, along with their children and livestock, into separate camps, so that in the event of attack, one camp might survive. He placed Leah's camp ahead of Rachel's, in the more vulnerable position. Upon encounter with Esau, Leah and Rachel bowed to him, and no harm was done to the family. We do not know how Leah died – only that she was buried in the cave at Machpelah with Jacob's forebears, in Canaan, facing Mamre.

VERSES

"And Laban had two daughters. The name of the elder was Leah and the name of the younger Rachel. And Leah's eyes were tender, but Rachel was comely in features and comely to look at, and Jacob loved Rachel."

—Genesis 29:16–18a

"And the LORD saw that Leah was despised and He opened her womb, but Rachel was barren. And Leah conceived and bore a son and called his name Reuben, for she said, "Yes, the LORD has seen my suffering, for now my husband will love me.""

—Genesis 29:31–32

"And Reuben went out during the wheat harvest and found mandrakes in the field and brought them to Leah his mother. And Rachel said to Leah, "Give me, pray, some of the mandrakes of your son." And she said, "Is it not enough that you have taken my husband, and now you would take the mandrakes of my son?" And Rachel said, Then let him lie with you tonight in return for the mandrakes of your son."

—Genesis 30:14–16

THEMES

Forbearance

To exercise forbearance sometimes means to "act as if" until our reality actually begins to change, and to bear up under a degree of internal discomfort in the meantime. Leah had to share her partner, Jacob, with her younger sister, Rachel, who entered their marriage only 7 days after it was consummated. (Some commentators explain that while Jacob worked another seven years in exchange for Rachel as his wife, the marriage itself took place at the end of one week.) Leah was well aware that Jacob loved Rachel more, yet she acted "as if," bearing her husband child after child and holding out faith that this would change his feelings for her. The name she chose for each child reflected both her internal discomfort with being unloved and her steady determination to change that reality. Among her sons were: Reuven ("Now my husband will love me");[1] Levi ("This time my husband will become attached to me");[2] and Zevulun ("This time my husband will exalt me").[3] Despite Leah's forbearance, Jacob demonstrates his continued preference for Rachel, placing Leah's camp in the more vulnerable position on the journey to Canaan. In death, however, Rachel is simply buried *b'derech* ("along the path") after dying in childbirth, while Leah is laid to rest in the Cave of Machpelah alongside Jacob's ancestors, where later Jacob, too, will lie beside her in perpetuity.

---

1. Gen. 30:32
2. Gen. 30:35
3. Gen. 30:20

MIDRASH

"That [Leah's eyes] were weak is not a disgrace, but a praise of her. For she would hear people talking at the crossroads, saying 'Rebecca has two sons and Lavan two daughters – the older [son] for the older, and the younger [son] for the younger. [Leah] would sit at the crossroads and ask: 'What are the deeds of the older?' 'He is an evil man who robs people.' 'What are the deeds of the younger?' 'He is a "quiet man, dwelling in tents"' (Gen. 25:27). So she would cry until her eyelashes fell out."

—Talmud Bavli, Bava Batra 123b

Our earliest introduction to Leah highlights her standout feature: her eyes. What exactly *einei Leah rakot*[1] means, however, is uncertain. Juxtaposed against the statement that follows, which extolls her sister Rachel's physical beauty, one might assume Leah's main characteristic to be a weakness; indeed, the phrase is often translated: "The eyes of Leah were weak." But *rach* can also mean soft, tender, youthful, or delicate. Could it be that there is an innocence to Leah – a sensitive, compassionate nature that is expressed through the look in her eyes? Rachel's beauty is manifest in her *physical* appearance, but perhaps Leah's eyes are the window to a beautiful *soul*.

This is the view of the sages, who say that it was Leah's great piety that Rachel envied,[2] not her fertility. They say that Leah's eyes were softened from the excessive tears she cried, thinking that as the older sister, she was fated to marry Jacob's older brother, Esau – understood by Leah to be a robber and a villain.[3] They say that Leah had such compassion for her sister's barrenness, that she prayed for one of her own children to be born female (Dinah), enabling Rachel to bear some of the twelve sons of Jacob that she knew would become the twelve tribes of Israel.[4] In the eyes of the sages, Leah was a woman of faith, prayer, and righteousness, who – though unloved and undervalued by her husband – was deserving of praise and rewarded by God. Her eyes were a window to a tender soul, which, at least in God's eyes, was every bit as beautiful as her sister's physical features.

---

1. Gen. 29:17
2. *Beresheet Rabbah* 71
3. *B. Bava Batra* 123a
4. *B. Berakhot* 60a

PROMPTS

In what realms of my life am I acting "as if"? What are the realities I would like to see change?

Have I ever succeeded in changing how someone feels about me?

Am I sacrificing too much for the sake of others' approval, or for my advancement in society?

Which events in my life have taught me resilience? Which have made me tender?

Rabbi Nicole K. Roberts is the first woman to be appointed senior rabbi in Australia. She has served the North Shore Temple Emanuel in Sydney since ordination in 2012 from the Hebrew Union College-Jewish Institute of Religion (Cincinnati), where she was awarded prizes for excellence in Mirdash and class standing. An alumna of the Tisch Rabbinical Fellowship, her writing has been published in the Prayers of Awe series (Rabbi Lawrence A. Hoffman, ed.) and in several "Rethinking" guides issued by Jewish Women International, on whose Clergy Task Force she serves. She is treasurer of the Council of Progressive Rabbis of Australia, New Zealand, and Asia and travels regularly to her country of origin, the United States, for conferences and family visits.

ROASTED EGGPLANT WITH TOMATO, ONION, AND ZA'ATAR

Leah's son finds "mandrakes" which Leah uses to barter for time with her husband. A member of the nightshade family, mandrakes are prevalent in the Mediterranean. (Nightshade vegetables contain calcitriol and alkaloids and include potatoes, tomatoes, eggplants and peppers.)

Our recipe elevates the humble eggplant, plain – and at times even bitter – with other elements from the nightshade family, to produce a warming, nutritious and versatile dish that will be the star on any dinner table. Use it as a dip, an accompaniment for roasted vegetables or as a sauce over pasta. It can be served hot or cold.

Prep time: 10 minutes

Cook time: 45 minutes

Serves: 4–6

Tools:

- Baking pan
- Knife
- Cutting board
- Large non-reactive sauté pan or Dutch oven

Ingredients:

- 2 large or 3 medium eggplants, cut in half lengthwise
- 1 medium yellow onion, peeled and diced
- 1 24 oz (680 g) can diced tomatoes, include liquid
- 1 tablespoon Za'atar spice blend
- 1 tablespoon olive oil or 2 tablespoons vegetable broth
- Sea salt or Kosher salt to taste

Instructions:

1. Preheat your oven to 375°F (190°C) and lightly oil a rimmed baking sheet.

2. Arrange the eggplants cut-side-up on the baking sheet and roast until tender, about 30 minutes.

3. While the eggplant is roasting, heat the olive oil or vegetable broth in a skillet over medium heat. Add the onions and cook until browned, around 5–6 minutes.

4. Add in the entire can of tomatoes and the za'atar seasoning, turn the heat down to low.

5. Remove the eggplant from the oven and scoop out the roasted flesh, discarding the skin. Roughly chop the eggplant flesh and add it to the skillet with the onions and tomatoes.

6. Give everything a good stir and taste and adjust the seasoning, adding more salt or za'atar, if necessary.

7. Serve immediately, with whole-grain bread and fresh vegetables, for dipping. The dip will last for up to a week in the fridge.

Elaine Taubin and Mary Cornelius met thirty-five years ago in Nashville, Tennessee where they were both working in the kitchen of a large hotel. Elaine's work as an executive chef took them all over the US. Mary has always been the primary cook at home where she put her early culinary training to good use. Now, as they near retirement, they have time to cook together at home and to get involved in various projects with their synagogue, including cooking for members of their community.

VEGAN CINNAMON DATE PECAN BABKA ROLLS

Leah represents a world of juxtapositions; inner beauty with a somewhat awkward exterior, always compared to her sister, loved but not quite as much as the next. The babka has a rich interior made from dried fruits or chocolate and an exterior that hides the inside. So, too, Leah was not a great beauty on the outside but her compassion and kindness ultimately shine through.

These vegan cinnamon date babka rolls require time for the savoury dough to rise. The light and airy finished texture will contrast with and complement the sweet filling. Regardless of your final presentation, they will taste delicious and be utterly satisfying.

Prep time: 3 hours
Cook time: 30 minutes
Serves: 12

Tools:

- Electric mixer with dough hook
- Food processor
- 2 × 18cm round cake pans or 2 × loaf pans
- Rolling pin
- Brush
- Scale
- Measuring spoons
- Knife

Ingredients:

For the dough:
- 4 cups (500 g) all-purpose flour
- 0.3 oz. (10 g) active dried yeast
- ¼ cup (60 ml) vegetable oil
- ½ cup + 1 tablespoon (140 g) applesauce
- ½ cup (120 ml) water
- 1 teaspoon vanilla extract
- Pinch of salt

For the filling:
- 1 cup (180 g) brown sugar
- 2 teaspoons ground cinnamon
- 2 oz. (60 g) medjool dates/ raisins/dried figs
- 3–4 tablespoons maple syrup
- 1 cup (100 g) pecans/walnuts

For the syrup:
- Date syrup
- Water

Instructions:

1. Place flour, yeast, oil, applesauce, water, salt, and vanilla into the bowl of an electric mixer with dough hook attached. Knead for 10–12 minutes or until dough is smooth and flexible.

2. Transfer the dough onto a lightly floured surface and use your hands to knead for another 1–2 minutes and form a ball. Transfer the dough into a lightly oiled bowl, cover with a tea-towel, and let it rise at room temperature for 60 minutes. It should double in volume.

3. Blend the dates (raisins/figs) in a food processor to form a paste. Set aside.

4. Blitz the pecans/walnuts in a food processor until they are broken down into small pieces. Add the brown sugar, cinnamon, and date (raisin/fig) paste to the food processor and blitz repeatedly, gradually adding the maple syrup in small amounts until the mixture loosely comes together. Set aside.

5. Divide the dough into two parts. On a floured surface, roll each part into a 4–5mm (¼-inch) thick rectangle.

6. Divide and spread the filling evenly over each rectangle. Roll each rectangle of dough into a tight cylinder. Cut into rolls and arrange on the separate cake pans.

7. Cover the pans with a tea-towel and let the rolls rise for 30–60 minutes. They should double in volume.

8. Preheat the oven to 335°F (170°C).

9. Dilute the date syrup with water to create a sticky syrup – recommended 1 part date syrup to 3 parts water.

10. Bake the rolls for 20 minutes

11. Remove from the oven and generously brush with the sticky date syrup.

12. Return into the oven and bake for a further 10 minutes, or until golden brown and slightly caramelized around the edges.

13. Cool slightly and serve at room temperature.

Zoe Singer is in her final year of school at Mount Scopus Memorial College in Melbourne, Australia. She is the School Captain of Jewish Life, and is involved in the local Jewish community.

DINAH

STORY

Dinah is the daughter of the patriarch Jacob. She is the youngest child of Jacob's wife, Leah, born after four sons. According to the biblical text, Dinah is Jacob's *only* daughter.

Dinah is known for her pivotal role in the story we might best call "The Shechem Affair." Genesis 34 recounts the relationship of the Hivite prince, Shechem, and Dinah, and its disastrous aftermath. The story as written is confusing and full of contradictions, and biblical scholars identify two independent narratives that are interwoven into the biblical text. (Traditional commentaries see this as one story with different perspectives.) In the first version, Dinah, perhaps ill advisedly, goes out to check out the local girls. Shechem sees her, abducts her and rapes her. When Dinah's brothers learn of the incident, they become enraged. Simeon and Levi kill Shechem and his father, and rescue Dinah.

In the alternative version of the story, Shechem becomes enamored of the new girl who moved into the neighborhood, and he commences to court her. Shechem's father approaches Dinah's family with a proposal of not only marriage, but an economic alliance between the two tribes. Jacob and sons agree to the arrangement with the proviso that Shechem and his entire clan adapt the Israelite practice of circumcision. Shechem eagerly institutes the agreement, but Dinah's brothers have something completely different in mind. Just as all Shechem's clan is weak from circumcision, the Israelites descend up on the town, massacre all of the men, and despoil the property.

The Torah tells us nothing else about Dinah's life, other than that she went down to Egypt with the rest of the family. The rabbis of the Midrash attempt to fill in some blanks. How or why did all this start? Because Jacob hid Dinah in the luggage so that his brother Esau would not see her and be attracted to her. What ever happened to Dinah? According to one account, she became the wife of Job.

VERSES

And Dinah, Leah's daughter, whom she had borne to Jacob, went out to go seeing among the daughters of the land. And Shechem, the son of Hamor the Hivvite, prince of the land, saw her and took her and lay with her and abused her."

—Genesis 34:1–2

"...and the men were pained and they were very incensed, for he had done a scurrilous thing in Israel by lying with Jacob's daughter, such as ought not to be done."

—Genesis 34:7

"And Hamor and Shechem his son they killed by the edge of the sword, and they took Dinah from the house of Shechem and went out...And they said, "Like a whore should our sister be treated?"

—Genesis 34:26–31

THEMES

Women navigating an inhospitable and dangerous world

No matter which Dinah narrative one finds more convincing, Dinah's attempt to engage the outside world, whether through her own initiative or by her passive existence, leaves her both defenseless and vulnerable to the actions of those around her. Ironically, both versions of the story suggest that in the end, as a woman, she has no choice. Whether Dinah is passive or active, all roads lead to a terrible and unhappy fate.

Women as passive observers of larger communal events

Dinah's concerns, desires and personal wishes are neither expressed nor considered. In fact, her voice is oddly absent. Nothing she does, or does not do, seems to have any effect on the arc of the story. As merely a token in the world of her father, brothers and other men, her status as a woman not only discounts any potential agency she might have but does not even allow us a window into her internal life.

The absence of women's sexual agency

Sexually Dinah is chosen. Sexually, Dinah is desired. Sexually, Dinah is taken. The story is devoid of Dinah's perspective, desire or reactions. Whether Dinah is interested, seduced, aroused or disgusted is completely missing and that perspective, one where a woman's sexuality seems to be irrelevant or completely beside the point, is the normative one in the Hebrew Bible.

MIDRASH

"That same night he arose, and taking his two wives, his two maidservants, and his eleven children, he crossed the ford of the Yabok." (Gen. 32:23) And where was Dinah? He put her in a chest and locked it, saying, "This evildoer should not see her and take her from me."

—Genesis *Rabbah* 76:9

Classic midrashim recount that when Jacob left for his famous showdown with Esau, he was concerned that Esau would claim Dinah as a wife. He therefore hid her in a locked trunk. This story echoes a similar story where Abraham, when he went down to Egypt, kept Sarah hidden in fear that the Pharaoh would take her if he were to see her (*Midrash Rabba - Bereishis*).

Commentary on the midrash suggests this behavior was not condoned and was seen a lack on the part of Jacob. Had Jacob allowed Esau to marry Dinah, Dinah may have transformed Esau into a good, God-fearing man. Instead he kept Dina sheltered, locked in a trunk, and, while saving Dinah, he lost Esau (Rashi on *Bereishis* 32:23 quoting *Bereishis Rabbah* 75:9).

What is striking about these stories (and the echo of the two stories is powerful in its repetition of a theme) is how much control is ascribed to a woman's sexuality, how powerful and how potentially dangerous it is seen as. While it is suggested as a catalyst for potential evil, it is also shown as a potential catalyst for redemption. Dinah's attractiveness and thus seductiveness, was considered to be so compelling that the only way to keep it under control it was to lock her in a trunk. Alternatively, her sexuality was so influential it would have caused Esau to repent; her sexuality and its power might have been so strong as to "turn" Esau away from his evil ways and seduce him to the light.

Perhaps a first step in re-approaching this midrash is to challenge the idea of sexuality as an all-powerful, uncontrollable force in our lives. A different reading would help people to understand that sex can be seen as a strong catalyst and driver but would not ascribe to it an overwhelming urge that cannot be harnessed. Dinah's sexuality should not be seen as a force so powerful that she or others will unwittingly act in response. Her beauty and sexuality should be seen as simply one element and characteristic of a young woman, and a part of the larger portrait of who she is.

Were we to approach Dinah as a young woman exploring her own sexuality, attempting to go out amongst other young women to learn about herself, perhaps she would be able to serve as a role model for today's young women exploring their own sexuality. Dinah may be portrayed as a woman who

was desired both by Esau and by Shechem, but she can also be portrayed as a woman who responded in kind to one of these men…or not. And perhaps she went on to develop a mutual relationship with another person with whom she was able to express her sexuality in a loving and positive context.

PROMPTS

Have you ever felt powerless in a situation in your family/at work/in society? How were you able to get your power back? Or how can you get your power back if a similar situation arises again?

Do you believe, in any way, that Dinah's brothers' actions were made with Dinah's best interests in mind? While our instinctive answer to that might be "no," is it possible for us to try to use a different cultural lens to see this more from the perspective of Dinah's brothers?

A later midrash suggests that Dinah married Job, a good and upright man who suffered terrible fates and still steadfastly believed in God. Why do you think the Midrash makes this pairing with Dinah? Are there a number of alternative ways to understand this?

Bat Sheva Marcus LCSW, MPH, PhD *is one of the founders and the Clinical Director of Maze Women's Sexual Health, one of the largest centers of its kind in the US. A profile in the NY Times magazine dubbed her "The Orthodox Sex Guru." Bat Sheva is a founder and past president of the Jewish Orthodox Feminist Alliance and has been involved in numerous local and national Jewish and feminist organizations. She has been profiled often in print magazines and has been a guest on numerous radio and television shows including CNBC, CBS News and Huffington Post Live.*

VEGAN CHOLENT

Dinah's experience of sexual violence will leave her shaken. Today, we could support Dinah by first taking her to the hospital, calling the police, and organizing psychotherapeutic support. We could commit to supporting her in the period that follows – staying by her side as she navigates the emotional and legal experience of sexual assault.

Appropriate nutrition is one of the things she needs to recover and heal. It is natural to offer food as a way of demonstrating love and care. If I was Dinah's mother, grandmother, sister or friend I would make this slow cooked Jewish stew in hopes that Dinah would drink its nourishing broth.

This is a veggie-centric version of cholent. You can make this cholent in a crock pot overnight.

Prep time: 8 hours

Cook time: 8 hours

Serves: 6–8

Tools:

- 1 small saucepan
- 1 large stew pot
- Vegetable peeler
- Box grater or julienne
- Nylon or cheesecloth bag

Ingredients:

- ⅔ cup (130 g) pearl barley
- 2 cups (500 ml) water
- 4 cups (225 g) fresh shiitake mushrooms, stems removed (or maitake mushrooms)
- 1 onion, diced
- 2 cups (150 g) sliced leeks or white part of green onions (½-inch pieces)
- 4 cloves garlic, minced
- 2 carrots, peeled and sliced (½-inch thick on a diagonal)
- 8 small yukon gold potatoes, peeled and chopped
- 1 cup (200 g) of raw kidney beans or butter beans or 2 cups cooked
- 6 cups (1.5 l) low-sodium vegetable broth
- 1 14-oz. can (400 g) diced tomatoes
- 4 bay leaves
- 2 teaspoons ground cinnamon
- ½ cup (125 ml) white wine
- Sea salt & pepper to taste
- Fresh parsley

Instructions:

1. Soak the raw beans for 8 hours. Drain and rinse under cold water; set aside.
2. Soak the pearl barley in 2 cups of water for 30 minutes.
3. Drain off excess water and place pearl barley in a fine mesh nylon bag (these are used to make nut milk) or cheesecloth bag and set aside.
4. Add all ingredients to the crock pot and pour the vegetable broth and canned tomatoes on top. Turn the crock pot on low.
5. Add the nylon mesh bag of pearl barley to the crock pot and cook for at least 8 hours.
6. Remove the nylon bag and put the barley into a bowl.
7. Place the soup and broth into a serving bowl with a lid.
8. Chop parsley and place in a small bowl for the table.
9. Let each person season to taste with fresh herbs, sea salt, and pepper.

From the Jewish Food Hero Kitchen

BEET AND CABBAGE SAUERKRAUT

There is an incredible Midrash (Jerusalem Talmud Berakhot 9:3) about Dinah that continues to capture my imagination.

Our tradition teaches us that Dinah, in fetus form in Leah's womb, was actually developing to be male. Leah knew that Jacob would be the father of twelve tribes. When she realized that she was with child and that Jacob already had ten sons (she had borne him six sons, Bilhah and Zilpah had each given birth to two sons), she said: Shall my sister Rachel not even be as one of the handmaidens? Leah therefore prayed to God on behalf of her sister, entreating Him: "Turn what is in my womb into a female, and do not prevent my sister from bearing a son." God accepted her prayer and the fetus in her womb was transformed into a girl.

I chose this recipe of beet and green cabbage sauerkraut as it shows the magic of transformation, through the fermentation process itself as well as the ombre effect from the rich color of the beets on the bottom seeping into the cabbage on top. This recipe is based on the sauerkraut recipe from the book Wild Fermentation by Sandor Elliz Katz.

Fermentation is a method of preserving food that dates back more than 2,000 years. During the fermentation process, beneficial probiotics or 'live bacteria' are produced, and these probiotics are what give sauerkraut most of its health benefits. This beet cabbage sauerkraut brings an incredible pop of color and flavor to any meal. Once you experience the magic of fermenting your own food you'll be hooked!

Prep time: 4 days–4 weeks (or more)
Cook time: assembly only
Serves: 4 cups/1 liter of sauerkraut

Tools:

- Small mixing bowl
- Large mixing bowl
- Food processor or grater
- One quart (4 cup) / 1 liter wide mouth mason jar

Ingredients:

- 1 small/medium beet (will be ½–1 cup when grated)
- 1 medium green cabbage (about 2lbs/900g)
- 1 scant tablespoon (14 g) Himalayan pink salt

Instructions:

1. Scrub and trim the beet but do not peel it.
2. Using a food processor and the fine to medium grater, grate the beet.
3. Pack the grated beet into the bottom of the mason jar. It should reach the 1 cup line on the mason jar, but no more than that.
4. Remove outer leaves from cabbage and set aside to use later.
5. Finely shred the cabbage using a food processor and the fine shredding attachment. (Alternatively you can also use a mandolin or just a large sharp knife).
6. Place shredded cabbage into a large mixing bowl and add the salt.
7. Massage/squeeze the salted cabbage with your hands or pound with a blunt tool for a few minutes until the juices start to release. You should be able to squeeze a handful and see the juices drip out (as from a wet sponge).
8. Pack the salted cabbage, along with all of its juices, into the mason jar on top of the grated beets.
9. Using your fingers, press the vegetables down with force so the air pockets are released and the juices rise to the top and cover the vegetables. Fill the jar not quite all the way to the top, leaving room for expansion.
10. Take one of the reserved outer cabbage leaves and fold it to fit inside the jar like a blanket, tightly tucking in the shredded vegetables below to prevent them from rising above the water.
11. Screw lid on and leave in a warm place in the kitchen. You might want to put a plate under the jar to protect your counters from potential leaking liquids.
12. Now all you have to do is wait! The fermentation process can take as little as three days or up to several months.
13. Every day loosen the lid to let out any gas build up and make sure that all of the shredded vegetables are still tucked in.
14. After three days you can start to taste your sauerkraut.
15. Shorter fermentation has a lighter flavor with a crisper texture. With longer fermentation the vegetables soften and the flavor continues to evolve. When the sauerkraut tastes "done" to you simply store it in your refrigerator, where it will last for many months.

Ketriellah Goldfeder is a Life Coach, Certified Hakomi Practitioner and founder of New Moon Coaching. For over two decades, she has provided therapeutic services which guide women on a path of mindful, embodied self discovery and personal growth. Her interest in natural cooking includes macrobiotic, raw and whole foods. She finds deep grounding and inspiration through her Jewish spiritual practice.

TAMAR

STORY

Tamar's story in the Hebrew Bible is one of being passed into the custody of man after man. Tamar is first taken by Judah as a wife for his eldest son, Er. After God kills Er for unspecified evil actions, Judah passes her into the custody of his second son, Onan, to fulfil the biblical obligation of *yibum*: levirate marriage. The Torah later commands that in the event that a man dies without children, his younger brother closest in age becomes responsible for conceiving a child with his widow, and a form of this legal construct was apparently customary prior to the biblical commandment. This child would be named the successor of the deceased. Yet Onan too is killed by God, for refusing to impregnate Tamar in avoidance of his levirate obligations.

Though legally she should be passed to Judah's next son, Shelah, to fulfil the obligation of *yibum*, Judah instead returns Tamar to her father's house for an indefinite amount of time. As Shelah's un-fulfilled levirate responsibility, Tamar is forbidden from marrying anyone else. Yet the text makes it clear that Judah never actually intends for Shelah to marry Tamar. Through all these events, Tamar does not take a single action. As time passes, she remains trapped in others' plans of inheritance and succession.

It is with a poignant sense of irony that Tamar gains agency through leaving the patriarchal structure. Prostitutes, as women without a specific male protector, were deemed the lowest, most vulnerable people in society. But Tamar, left with no other prospect of bearing children, dons the guise of a prostitute and seduces her father-in-law, Judah.

The text describes how "she covered herself with a veil and wrapped herself," such that when Judah saw her, "he took her for a whore, for she had covered her face." Though perhaps the implication of the text, it is hard to imagine that her face remained covered for the remainder of their interac-tion. This leads the midrash to interpret the phrase "for she had covered her face," as referring not to Tamar's appearance at the crossroads but to her usual standard of modesty. Since her face was *always* covered, Judah "did not see her all of the days that she lived in his house, therefore he did not recognize her" (Rashi, Sotah 10b).

As collateral for the payment she never plans to receive, Tamar takes Judah's seal-and-cord and staff, symbols of clan leadership. Tamar takes symbolic ownership of the very power which previously repressed her. Even as Tamar deserts her prescribed place in the social order, she hints that Judah deserves to be demoted as well. She traded the garments of her widowhood for the scarf of a prostitute; he too abdicates the symbols of his masculine dominance.

Three months later, Tamar is discovered to be pregnant. Judah sentences her to death for apparent adultery. Now, however, Tamar no longer acts submissively. She challenges Judah to admit to being the father, displaying his seal-and-cord and staff as proof. Judah acknowledges her righteousness; she acted out of desperation in a situation in which he himself had placed her.

The narrative concludes with Tamar birthing not one but two male heirs from her union with Judah. The Torah traces the lineage of her eldest twin through the Book of Ruth until the birth of King David. In spite of the men around her trying to secure their genealogical succession, Tamar is ultimately the person responsible for engineering the Messianic line.

VERSES

"And Judah said to Tamar his daughter-in-law, "Stay a widow in your father's house until Shelah my son is grown up," for he thought, Lest he, too, die like his brothers. And Tamar went and stayed at her father's house."

—Genesis 38:11

"And she took off her widow's garb and covered herself with a veil and sat by the entrance to Enaim, which is on the road to Timnah, for she saw that Shelah had grown up and she had not been given to him as a wife. And Judah saw her and took her for a whore, for she had covered her face."

—Genesis 38:14–15

"Out she was taken, when she sent to her father-in-law, saying, "By the man to whom these belong I have conceived," and she said, "Recognize, pray, whose are this seal-and-cord and this staff?" And Judah recognized them and he said, "She is more right than I, for have I not failed to give her to Shelah, my son?""

—Genesis 38:25–26

THEMES

Subversion

Tamar transforms her circumstances. At the beginning of her life, she conforms to social and legal expectations without resistance or complaint. However, once she realizes that the male authority to whom she has submitted abandoned and trapped her, she acts through the only means available to her: subversion. Tamar consciously abandons her sanctioned role, utilizing her once-restrained sexuality as a means to take ownership of her fate.

Strategic timing

Patience, precision, and perhaps a little Divine providence enable Tamar to make the perfect moves at the perfect time. She stations herself at the crossroad exactly as Judah passes by, evidently at the right point of her fertility cycle. She requests Judah's most identifying objects at the moment when he can't refuse. She defends herself against Judah's accusations of adultery at the most public moment, so that he can't dismiss her proof. Tamar is a woman very attuned to time.

MIDRASH

בשלמא אונן דכתיב ביה ושחת ארצה אלא ער מנלן אמר רב נחמן בר יצחק דכתיב (בראשית לח, י) וימת גם אותו אף הוא באותו מיתה מת בשלמא אונן משום לא לו יהיה הזרע אלא ער מ"ט עבד הכי כדי שלא תתעבר ויכחיש יפיה.

"So that she would not become pregnant and mar her beauty".

—*Yevamot* 34b

The text states that Tamar's first husband, Er, was killed for "committing evil in God's eyes," but does not account the specific nature of his wrongdoing. The *Gemara* (*Yevamot* 34b) suggests that Er committed the same sin as Onan: he refused to have sex with Tamar in a way which would impregnate her.

Onan's motivation for preventing Tamar's pregnancy is explicit. The laws of levirate marriage clearly state that the child of their sexual union would not be attributed to him, but would instead inherit from his deceased brother. Onan wanted his biological children to belong to him alone. Additionally, if Er remained without an heir, Onan would likely have inherited all his older brother's property. It is for this utter selfishness that God killed Onan. These motivations, however, would not apply to Er.

Why did Er withhold his seed from Tamar? "So that she would not become pregnant and mar her beauty." Er controlled Tamar sexually and reproductively for his carnal pleasure.

This midrash acknowledges a very particular paragon of female beauty: the pristine, untouched, eternally youthful, virginal woman. An ephemeral ideal, the moment of early womanhood naturally ends as time passes and women's bodies and experiences evolve. Yet it is the beauty ideal promoted by modern culture that almost perfectly encapsulates the feminist concept of "the male gaze"; representations of women as sexual objects for the pleasure of the male viewer.

The Rabbis were clearly not on board with this perception of female beauty. They unequivocally categorize Er's attempt to maintain his wife's untouched appearance through sexual and reproductive manipulation as a sin. A sin so wrong, it was punished by death.

In this midrash, the similarities between Er and Onan run deeper than their act of sin; both are motivated by extreme self-centeredness. They treat Tamar as a vessel of pleasure, audaciously disregarding her as a participant in the sexual and reproductive process. This too, is an attitude depicted negatively in the rabbinic literature.

Throughout rabbinic literature, there are competing opinions on the value of mutually pleasurable sexual engagement. The rabbinic interpretation of this narrative could be read to substantively support the inclusion of women in partnered sexual encounters. This voice resonates with the cry of modern women advocating for agency in their own reproductive and sexual experiences.

PROMPTS

Throughout the narrative, much negotiation swirls around Tamar's body, particularly its reproductive capacity. Who has a voice in discussions relating to my reproductive capacity? Whose voice do you want to hear? Whose voices do you not welcome in this discussion?

The Messianic line emerges from Tamar and Judah's questionable sexual union. This theme continues in the Torah: Ruth & Boaz and David & Batsheva also conceived a link in the messianic line through questionable sexual unions. In what way might it be significant that the lineage of the Davidic monarchy, and therefore Messiah, flows through non-standard sexual unions? What might that imply about the significance of a certain kind of 'bloodline purity' in Jewish thought?

It is important to note that for the modern reader, this story raises questions of consent. In addition to Tamar being the victim of sexual control and manipulation, she herself seems to sexually manipulate Judah; Judah evidently did not know the true identity of the woman with whom he was having sex. Was Tamar justified in withholding information and thereby sexually manipulating Judah?

Ora Weinbach is a graduate student at Yale Divinity School, a participant in the Wexner Graduate Fellowship, and the Community Educator at The Jewish Center in Manhattan. She holds a BA in Jewish Education from Yeshiva University where she was a Legacy Heritage Fellow. She taught Limmudei Qodesh for seven years at the Abraham Joshua Heschel High School. Ora currently teaches human sexuality to both teens and parents and consults with Jewish day schools on sexuality education. In the summers, Ora serves as the Director of Student Life at the Tikvah Summer High School Institute hosted at Yale University.

BAKED SWEET POTATO MEDITERRANEAN NACHOS

If Tamar had conformed to biblical ideas about widows, she would have lived a marginalised life. Instead, she takes control of changing her own circumstances.

We can learn from Tamar that we don't have to accept our current circumstances and societal norms. We can forge our own path and do what we believe to be right. Many women today feel food is a struggle as we live in a culture surrounded by unhealthy food and eating habits. But like Tamar we can take control of our own life.

Nachos are a northern Mexican dish which have become a popular comfort food in America, piled high with meat and cheese. I wanted to create a healthier alternative, a delicious dish which brings comfort and is also healing for our bodies.

These sweet potato nachos come with all the trimmings – crunchy potatoes, hearty chickpeas, tangy cheese sauce, and herby salsa. These are healthy and tasty nachos that you can actually feel good about eating.

Prep time: 15 minutes
Cook time: 30 minutes
Serves: 4

Tools:

- Large knife
- Baking sheet
- Parchment paper
- Large and small prep bowls
- Cutting board
- Measuring cups
- Spoons

Ingredients:

- 4 sweet potatoes, cut into thick wedges, skin on
- 2 tablespoons olive oil (or oil of choice)
- 1 cup (200 g) grain of choice (wheat berries or farro work well)
- 1 15-oz. (425 g) can chickpeas, rinsed and drained
- 1 teaspoon ground cumin
- ½ teaspoon chili powder and/or smoked paprika
- ½ cup (75 g) cherry tomatoes, halved
- 2 English cucumbers, chopped
- ½ cup parsley, chopped
- Juice of ½ a lemon
- 2 tablespoons olive oil
- Salt and pepper to taste

For the "cheese" tahini sauce:
- ½ cup (110 g) tahini
- 1 garlic clove, minced
- 1 lemon, juiced
- 1 tablespoon miso paste
- ½ teaspoon ground turmeric
- ¼ cup (60 ml) water or unsweetened almond milk

Instructions:

1. Preheat your oven to 400°F (200°C) degrees and line a baking sheet with a piece of parchment paper.

2. In a large mixing bowl, toss the sweet potato wedges with olive oil and a fat pinch of salt and pepper to taste. Arrange on the prepared baking sheet and roast until golden brown and slightly crispy around the edges, around 25–30 minutes, flipping halfway through.

3. Remove from the oven and set aside to cool.

4. In the same bowl you used to toss the sweet potatoes, add the chickpeas, ground cumin, and chili powder. Season with salt and pepper to taste. Toss the chickpeas and transfer to a greased baking sheet. Roast until golden brown, around 20 minutes.

5. While the sweet potatoes and chickpeas are roasting, bring 2 cups (500 ml) of water to a boil in a medium pot and add the grains.

6. Simmer the grains until cooked through, around 20 minutes. Drain and set aside in mixing bowl.

7. Once the chickpeas are done, remove from the oven and add to the cooked grains. Season with a fat pinch of salt and pepper. This will act as your meat layer.

8. To make the salsa, in a medium-sized bowl, combine cherry tomatoes, cucumber, parsley, lemon juice, chili powder, and olive oil. Season with salt and pepper to taste and gently stir all ingredients together. Set aside to marinate.

9. To prepare the cheese sauce, add all ingredients, except the water/almond milk, to a small mixing bowl and stir to combine. Slowly add the water/almond milk until the sauce reaches a pourable consistency that resembles cheese sauce.

10. To assemble, arrange the sweet potato wedges in a circle on a plate. Top with the chickpea/grain mixture, followed by the salsa, and finally drizzle the "cheese" tahini sauce on top.

11. Share the plate with a few friends or serve onto individual plates.

Julie Podair is a classically trained biochemist turned tech recruiter, now a full-time personal chef based out of San Francisco, CA. As a scientist at heart, Julie is constantly experimenting with new flavors and ingredients to create nourishing recipes for a wide range of diets. Her mission is to show people that healthy food can taste delicious, no matter the diet.

CHOCOLATE HAZELNUT TRUFFLES

Tamar's shrewdness is manifested in her capacity to disguise herself and reveal her identity at just the right time and in the right way. Like her, these chocolate truffles appear one way on the outside, concealing something altogether different within.

These are some seriously decadent chocolate and hazelnut truffles that you won't believe are vegan and made with healthy ingredients. The hazelnuts are rich in magnesium and B vitamins and also work as the crunchy element in these melt-in-the-mouth chocolate truffles.

Prep time: 15 minutes
Cook time: assembly only
Serves: 8–10

Tools:

- Food processor
- 2 medium mixing bowls
- Spatula
- Baking Sheet
- Parchment paper
- Measuring cups
- Tablespoon and teaspoon measuring cups

Ingredients:

- 2 large avocados, peeled and pitted
- 3 oz. (90 g) vegan chocolate chips, melted
- 4 tablespoons pure maple syrup, divided
- 4 tablespoons cocoa powder, divided
- ½ cup (50 g) almond flour
- ¼ teaspoon coarse sea salt
- 16 whole hazelnuts
- 4 tablespoons coconut oil, liquid state at room temperature

Instructions:

1. In the bowl of a food processor, combine the avocadoes, melted chocolate, 2 tablespoons of maple syrup, 2 tablespoons of cocoa powder, almond flour, and sea salt. Pulse until completely smooth and creamy, with no green specks from the avocado, around a minute or two.

2. Transfer the avocado chocolate mixture to a medium mixing bowl and place in the freezer for 20 minutes or until the mixture is firm.

3. Line a large baking sheet with parchment paper. Remove the avocado mixture from the freezer and using a tablespoon measure, scoop out 16 truffles from the mixture and transfer to the baking sheet.

4. Place a hazelnut into each of the 16 truffles and using slightly wet hands, roll into even balls. Arrange all truffles on the baking sheet and place in the freezer for another 15 minutes.

5. In a separate mixing bowl, combine the liquid coconut oil with 2 tablespoons of cocoa powder and 2 tablespoons of maple syrup. Whisk until completely smooth and glossy.

6. Using 2 forks, dip each truffle into the chocolate sauce and place back on the baking sheet. Once all the truffles are coated with the chocolate sauce, transfer back into the freezer for another 15 minutes or until the chocolate coating is set.

7. Store chilled for up to 1 week.

From the Jewish Food Hero Kitchen

SHIFRA

STORY

Shifra was a midwife who, alongside Puah, was responsible for delivering the babies of the Israelites in Egypt in the time of Pharaoh. Feeling threatened, Pharaoh ordered the midwives to kill all male babies born to the Israelites. Shifra and Puah directly defied Pharoah's order and allowed the babies to live, thereby giving life to an entire generation of male Israelites. For their bravery, fearlessness, commitment to life and goodness, the Torah tells us that God rewarded Shifra and Puah.

VERSES

"And the king of Egypt said to the Hebrew midwives, one of whom was named Shiphrah and the other was named Puah. And he said, "When you deliver the Hebrew women and look on the birth-stool, if it is a boy, you shall put him to death, and if it is a girl, she may live."

—Exodus 1:15–16

"And the king of Egypt called the midwives and said to them, "Why did you do this thing and let the children live?" And the midwives said to Pharaoh, "For not like the Egyptian women are the Hebrew women, for they are hardy. Before the midwife comes to them they give birth."

—Exodus 1:18–19

"And God made it go well with the midwives, and the people multiplied and became very vast. And inasmuch as the midwives feared God, He made households for them."

—Exodus 1: 20–21

THEMES

Civil Disobedience

Shifra and Puah's defiance of Pharoah's orders is the first act of civil disobedience in the Torah. They recognized the inherent wrong being enacted by the all-powerful ruler and chose to disobey him.

They defied him not through violent means but by life-giving actions. They set a model for how we might respond when we see leaders perpetuating great injustice and inflicting harm on society.

Bravery

Shifra and Puah not only defy the King's orders but when he questions them, they dare to answer back. It is difficult to act in defiance, all the more so when it means putting one's own life at risk. Shifra serves as a role model for standing up for what one believes, for doing what is right, and for acting bravely and with courage.

Female Solidarity

We learn in the *Talmud* of *Massechet* (Tractate) Sota that the Jewish people were redeemed from Egypt on the merits of the righteous women of that generation. Shifrah and Puah were among those righteous women, bravely delivering babies that had been condemned by Pharaoh to death. There is perhaps no greater embodiment of female solidarity than the midwife whose strength, compassion, love, and a deep understanding of the female body allows her to brings new life safely into the world.

MIDRASH

"They let them live": Rashi writes, "They provided them with food." This is difficult, where does Rashi get this from? You could say that he sees something superfluous in the text. After "They did not do as the King of Egypt told them," there was no need to write, "And they let the boys live." Rather, it comes to teach us something new, that they supplied them with food in addition to the fact that they did not kill them.

—Obadiah ben Abraham Bartenura, Exodus 1:17

Rashi and the Bartenura pick up on a seeming redundancy in our story. If the Torah tells us that Shifra and Puah did not follow Pharoah's order to kill the babies, why does the Torah then need to specify that they let them live? Clearly, they let them live if they did not kill them! Rather, Rashi and the Bartenura teach, this phrase must come to tell us something new: quite literally that Shifra and Puah gave life to these newly born babies. Refusal to kill required only that they *not* take action, but they went above and beyond this moral call to duty. After they provided the babies with the nourishment they needed. They provided them with food and water.

Shifra's name is connected to the Hebrew root *shin-peh-resh* which means to improve or beautify. She delivers babies into the world and beautifies them, cleaning them, holding them, helping them to take their first breaths. Shifra's story is one that calls on us to stand up for what we know to be right, even when that requires defying those who are in power. Her story teaches us not to respond passively but rather to take action, going above and beyond the call to help as we care for the physical and emotional nourishment of those in need.

PROMPTS

Where in your life do you need some of Shifra's bravery? What is stopping you from taking action?

Who do you feel called to protect? How can you step forward as Shifra did?

What are you willing to stand up for at the expense of your own comfort and convenience?

Who are the female role models that inspire you to action?

Rabbi Avi Strausberg is the Director of National Learning Initiatives at Hadar, and based in Washington, DC. Previously, she served as the Director of Congregational Learning of Temple of Aaron in St. Paul, Minnesota. She received her rabbinic ordination from Hebrew College in Boston and is a Wexner Graduate Fellow. Energized by engaging creatively with Jewish text, she has written several theatre pieces inspired by the Torah and maintains a Daf Yomi haiku blog in which she writes daily Talmudic haikus. Avi is most grateful for her wife Chana and two children Ori and Niv.

LUDMILLA'S CAULIFLOWER AND BEAN SOUP

The story of Shifra reminded me of Ludmilla, my 'adopted grandmother,' a Jewish widow in St. Petersburg who used her meager pension for a weekly trip to the farmer's market to collect vegetables for her beloved soups.

Ludmilla, like Shifra, lived a life of inner strength and bravery. As a child, she survived the Siege of Leningrad, being orphaned, starvation and pogroms. As an adult, she endured the murder of her only child and the deaths of two cherished husbands. Like Shifra, though she was forever confronting emotional, political, physical, and economic turmoil, Ludmilla always found her inner strength to carry on, surrounding herself with her intellectual Jewish friends even in times when identifying as Jewish was both dangerous and illegal. This soup is symbolic of the comfort that Ludmilla found in simplicity and consistency.

This is a comforting soup. Ludmilla would make it weekly, and we would eat it together every night with rye bread. This is a full-proof recipe, you can't go wrong with it, and you can take liberties with quantities. It is simple to make, filling, and delicious!

Prep time: 15 minutes
Cook time: 1 hour
Serves: 6–8

Tools:

- Cutting Board
- Sharp Knife
- 16 Qt. Pot
- Bowls or Containers to separate chopped vegetables
- Measuring cups and spoons

Ingredients:

- 4 tablespoons olive oil
- 1 medium onion, diced
- 6 carrots, diced
- 2 peppers, diced (yellow, red, orange)
- 1–2 cloves garlic, minced
- 2 teaspoons kosher salt
- 3 tablespoons tomato paste
- 4 32-oz. boxes of vegetable broth (3.78 l) or water with vegetable bouillon cube or homemade vegetable broth
- ½ cup (90 g) brown rice (optional)
- 1 large cauliflower, split into small florets
- 1 15-oz. (425 g) can cannellini or white beans (if using dried beans, soak in water the night before and rinse well)

Instructions:

1. Heat olive oil in a large soup pot over medium heat.
2. Add the onions and cook, stirring occasionally, until the onion becomes soft and translucent, around 8–10 minutes.
3. Add the carrots and cook, stirring occasionally, for an additional 5 minutes. Season with ½ teaspoon of salt.
4. Add the peppers, cook for an additional 5 minutes. Season with another ½ teaspoon of salt.
5. Add garlic and continue cooking for another minute, just until the garlic becomes fragrant.
6. Stir in the tomato paste, making sure it coats all the vegetables.
7. Add in the brown rice, if using, and pour in the vegetable broth. Bring to a boil.
8. Stir in the cauliflower florets and bring the heat down to medium-low. Let the soup simmer away for 25–30 minutes.
9. Finally, add in the beans and simmer for another 10–15 minutes. Taste and adjust the seasoning before serving.
10. Garnish with parsley, dill or both.

Jennifer Alfond Seeman received a BA from Colby College in Russian/Soviet Studies in 1992. She was awarded the Condon Medal and a Watson Fellowship. Jenny taught citizens' initiative and environmental studies in Russia during her Watson year. Following this, she remained in St. Petersburg and worked for McKinsey & Company. Jenny is engaged in education and serves on multiple higher education boards. Jenny is passionate about family and food and comes from many generations of women who see food as love. Jenny and her husband Tom have four children.

VEGAN KIBBEH NAYYEH

When Shifra saved baby boys from Pharaoh's edict, she didn't just let them live, she kept them alive: she fed and took care of them. This recipe is satiating and leaves you feeling nourished, just like Shifra's care.

These Kibbeh Nayyeh are fresh, simple to make and healthy. This is a vegan adaptation of my great grandmother's Kibbeh Neye, a spiced raw meat spread. This vegan version has two main ingredients: lentils and wheat. I have added a couple of extra vegetables prepared in the Catalan style to honor my current home.

Prep time: 1 hour

Cook time: 1 hour

Serves: 4–6

Tools

- Food processor
- Colander
- Chopping board
- Chopping knife
- Pan
- Small bowl
- Large mixing bowl
- Tray
- Tea spoon
- Wooden spoon
- Newspaper

Ingredients:

- 1 cup (200 g) lentils, rinsed and drained
- ½ cup (100 g) bulgur wheat
- 1 red pepper
- 1 eggplant
- 1 onion, chopped
- ¼ cup (60 g) parsley
- ¼ cup (60 g) basil (60g)
- ¼ cup (60 g) mint (60g)
- 1 teaspoon smoked paprika
- 1 teaspoon seven spices
- 1 teaspoon cumin
- ½ lemon
- 1 hot pepper, chopped (optional)
- 4 tablespoons extra-virgin olive oil
- 2 cups (500 ml) water
- 18 crisp Romaine lettuce leaves
- salt and pepper to taste

Instructions:

1. Preheat your oven to 480°F (250°C) degrees.

2. Once the oven temperature reaches 480°F (250°C) reduce to 350°F (180°C) degrees.

3. Roast the red pepper and eggplant until soft and cooked through, turning occasionally, around 40 minutes. Remove from the oven and wrap with a newspaper. Set aside for 20 minutes.

4. Being careful not to get burned, peel the eggplant and peel and deseed the pepper. Slice the vegetables lengthwise and transfer into a bowl with a pinch of salt and a tablespoon of olive oil. Set aside.

5. Place the bulgur wheat in a small bowl and cover with hot water. Set aside for 1 hour.

6. Heat one tablespoon of olive oil in a frying pan over medium heat. Add the onion and the lentils; cook, stirring occasionally, until the lentils turn lighter in color.

7. Add the water and let the lentils cook until they are soft. Add more water if necessary.

8. Drain the bulgur and mix it with the cooked lentils, parsley, mint, basil, paprika, seven spices, cumin, lemon juice, salt to taste, and the remaining two tablespoons of olive oil (and the hot pepper if you want to use it).

9. Serve on a plate alongside the roasted eggplant and peppers. To eat, use the lettuce leaves as a spoon. You can also use pita bread.

Mónica Buzali Kalach is Syrian-Jewish woman, born in México and currently living in Barcelona. She has a Catalan husband, and is mother to Daniela and Elías. Her greatest hobby is cooking. She is the co-owner of Toldot Barcelona, a project that shares Jewish culture through food and honours all the women who have been feeding us through time. Mónica volunteers for Mozaika, a platform that promotes Jewish culture in the heart of Barcelona.

ZIPPORAH

STORY

Zipporah is the wife of Moses, the main character in four of the five books in the Hebrew Bible, and she is largely a mystery. Her origins as the eldest daughter of Jethro, the Midianite priest, are established in the second chapter of Exodus. It is to Midian that Moses flees after killing an Egyptian slavemaster.

Zipporah and Moses meet, like so many Biblical couples, at a well. He comes to her rescue, defying the shepherds who turn her and her sisters away. Here Zipporah falters; rather than inviting Moses back to her father's house as ancient Near Eastern hospitality dictates, she leaves him there only for Jethro to order her back to retrieve him. With nary an introduction, Jethro gives Zipporah to Moses as his wife. Only upon becoming *his* wife do we learn *her* name.

As a character, Zipporah would likely remain underdeveloped were it not for two infamously challenging verses in Exodus chapter four. After encountering God at the burning bush, Moses is called upon to redeem the Israelites from slavery in Egypt. He protests initially and finally submits, heading back to Egypt with Zipporah and their sons in tow. En route, in the dark of night at their encampment, God attempts to kill Moses. Zipporah intervenes, taking a piece of flint in hand, circumcising her son and touching the foreskin to his legs.

The verses are terse, bizarre and painfully opaque. Why does God want to kill Moses? Which son does Zipporah circumcise? What does God find appeasing about Zipporah's violent, unexpected intervention? What we do know is that this time, Zipporah does not falter. This time, *she* comes to *his* rescue. As a result of her actions, God departs and Moses survives, continuing on to confront Pharaoh.

We don't hear about Zipporah again until after the exodus from Egypt. Zipporah is mentioned almost in passing as Jethro travels with her and her two sons to meet Moses in the wilderness. Does Moses ask for Zipporah? Did she request to be reunited? We don't know. But it's worth noting that despite this somewhat lackluster final appearance, the Torah isn't given at Mount Sinai until after Moses and Zipporah are reunited. Perhaps Moses needs Zipporah in the blinding light of revelation as much as he did in the dark of night.

VERSES

"And he said to his daughters, "And where is he? Why did you leave the man? Call him that he may eat bread." And Moses agreed to dwell with the man, and he gave Zipporah his daughter to Moses. And she bore a son, and he called him Gershom, for he said, "A sojourner have I been in a foreign land."

—Exodus 2:20–22

"And it happened on the way in the night camp that the LORD encountered him and sought to put him to death. And Zipporah took a flint and cut off her son's foreskin and touched it to his feet, and she said, "Yes, a bridegroom of blood you are to me.""

—Exodus 4:24–26

"And Jethro, Moses' father-in-law, took Zipporah, Moses' wife, after her being sent away, and her two sons, one of whom was named Gershom, for he said, "A sojourner I have been in a foreign land," and the other was named Eliezer, "For the God of my fathers was my aid and rescued me from Pharaoh's sword.""

—Exodus 18:2–4

THEMES

The movement from passive to active:

Zipporah's story presents her first as a woman who things are happening to. As the story evolves she becomes a woman who is connected to her own personal agency and takes decisive action. Finally, she is presented as someone who makes things happen.

Wife as protector:

Zipporah is shown as a wife who preserves the life of her husband and, by extension, the Jewish people. Without her, Moses would not have survived to lead the Israelites out of Egypt.

Relational identity and social constraints:

This biblical narrative points to the social constraints that manifest from Zipporah's relational identity – she is Jethro's daughter, Moses' wife, Gershom and Eliezer's mother… but who is *she*?

MIDRASH

[Jethro] gave me his daughter Zipporah as a wife on the condition that all children born in my house would be half-Jewish and half-Ishmaelite.

—*Midrash Vayosha 4*

Zipporah is a heroine, but she is not a Jewish heroine. She is the pagan daughter of Jethro, the Midianite priest. In several classical interpretations of her story (*Midrash Vayosha 4*, *Yashar Shemot* 141b-142a), the sages teach that Jethro approved of her marriage to Moses only if they would agree to raise their children between the two faiths: half of the children according to Midianite polytheism and half according to Israelite monotheism. As such, when Gershom was born, Moses circumcised him. But when their second son, Eliezer was born, he was not circumcised. At the night encampment when God comes for Moses, Zipporah dismisses Jethro's condition and proactively chooses the Israelite faith, and along with it circumcision, for her second son.

The tension around intermarriage was present for Moses and Zipporah. It persists today. Many Jewish people choose partners who were brought up in, or who currently practice, other faiths. Some intermarry without strife, but for others it is intensely painful. A modern reading of Zipporah's choice to raise her sons outside of her faith of origin casts her in a powerful light. She was the daughter of a priest, a leader of the Midianite faith, yet she was able to circumcise her second son in a crystallising moment of transition for her family.

We need not infer from this midrash that Zipporah abandoned her culture when she decided to raise her children in the Jewish faith. We can imagine that the culture in which she was born and raised influenced her, Moses, and their sons.

From Zipporah we see an example of a woman who sets the tone for the family. Zipporah could have chosen to follow her father's directive of raising the children with double faith, but she saw that Judaism was going to define the life of her family and chose it for all of them. Women today are pivotal in deciding what faith their children will be brought up in, and they should put aside the fears of what other family members will say, or what society will say, and make the choice that is right for their own particular family.

PROMPTS

Why is Zipporah depicted as needing rescuing when her character is first introduced? How does this initial characterization impact her character's arc moving forward?

Zipporah is often framed by the men around her: her father, her husband, her sons. But when we first meet her, we learn that she is one of seven sisters. In what ways might considering her as an older sister shape the way you think about her as a daughter, wife, mother?

In traditional Jewish practice, women do not perform circumcisions. What does this story teach us about women's roles as ritual practitioners? How might Zipporah's story inspire our own approach to ritual?

Rabbi Jessica Minnen is the Director of Jewish Learning and Rabbi in Residence at OneTable, a national initiative that invites young adults in their 20s and 30s to end their week with intention at the Shabbat dinner table. She believes that stepping back, connecting with others, having moments of mindfulness, and enjoying great meals on a Friday night is important... and just might change your life. Originally from Paducah, Kentucky, Jessica is an alumna of Washington University in St. Louis, the Pardes Institute of Jewish Studies, Paideia: The European Institute for Jewish Studies in Sweden, Baltimore Hebrew University, and the Jewish Theological Seminary.

CHINESE TOFU MATZO BALLS IN TIANJIN SWEET AND SOUR SAUCE

I imagine that Zipporah's cooking and eating was impacted by her Midianite background in a new land, just as my cooking and eating was influenced by the food and culture of China, where I was born and lived until I was 18. In China, soybean is considered a sacred plant and soybean curd (tofu) is a staple food. These Chinese tofu matzo balls have been a regular dish on our Seder table at Pesach for vegans and for those who don't like fishy gefilte fish! This recipe was from my late husband, Jim z"l, who was also born in Harbin. He was an industrial chemist and engineer who was a very creative chef, especially in vegetarian cooking.

Prep time: 45 minutes
Cook time: 20–40 minutes (depending on cooking method)
Serves: 6–8

Tools:

- Cutting board
- Knife
- Fork
- Measuring cups and spoons
- Mixing bowl
- Baking tray
- Frying pan

Ingredients:

For the tofu balls:
- 1 14-oz. (400 g) box of medium soft tofu
- 1 cup (125 g) of fine matzo meal
- 4 spring onions, white part only
- 1 tablespoon sesame oil
- 3 garlic cloves, finely chopped
- 1 thumb-sized ginger piece, finely chopped
- 2 tablespoons soy sauce

For the sweet and sour sauce:
- 6 tablespoon red Chinese vinegar
- 4 tablespoon sugar
- 4 tablespoon light soy sauce
- 4 thumb-sized ginger piece, finely chopped
- 3 garlic cloves, finely chopped
- 2 spring onions, finely chopped
- Vegetable oil, for frying

Instructions:

1. In a large mixing bowl, mash tofu with a fork until mostly smooth. Add in the remaining ingredients and stir to combine.
2. Lightly oil your hands with sesame oil and roll the tofu mixture into small balls. Lay the tofu balls on a tray and set aside to rest for 30 minutes.
3. To cook the tofu balls, either fry in an oiled pan or bake for 30–40 minutes in an oven preheated to 375°F (190°C) degrees.
4. To make the sweet and sour sauce, heat a small amount of vegetable oil in a wok or frying pan. Add in the garlic, ginger, and spring onions; stir-fry for 1 minute.
5. Add in the remaining ingredients and continue frying until the sugar is dissolved and everything is well-combined, around a minute or two.
6. Serve the tofu balls alongside the sweet and sour dipping sauce.

Nora Vinson is an Australian-Jewish great grandmother who was born in Harbin, China, and grew up in the British Concession in Tianjin (known as Teintsin at that time). Her parents' family had migrated to China from Russia in the 1920s after the Russian Revolution. She migrated to Melbourne Australia when she was 18 years old, after Chairman Mao's Communist rule began. She is Yin & Yang; she is East meets West; she is a woman of the world who embraces all people and cultures and believes that love is the answer.

EVERYTHING BAGEL EDAMAME RICE BOWL (DONBURI)

Like Zipporah, many of us who were not born Jewish find ourselves at a crossroads: does embracing Judaism mean leaving behind our faiths and customs of origin? Days before I faced the beit din (Jewish court) at my conversion, I almost backed out. What if Judaism completely overshadowed my already seemingly distant Japanese heritage? (I am a fourth generation Japanese American). Our rabbi responded: "Why can't there be room for both?" There is room for both and so much more. My devotion to Judaism has only gotten deeper with my dedication to my Japanese American heritage and vice versa.

This recipe was one of my earliest blended recipes. Instead of a bagel, the base is rice ("donburi" means rice bowl). I've swapped in edamame for the protein instead of salmon, and avocado in place of cream cheese. The colorful toppings make it rich in vitamins, minerals, and healthy fats. I'd like to think that Zipporah and Moses would have cooked blended Jewish and Midianite recipes for their sons, too!

Prep time: 40 minutes

Cook time: 75 minutes

Serves: 5–6

Tools:

- Chopping board
- Chef's knife
- Rice cooker or large pot for cooking rice
- Cookie sheet
- Mason jar or bowl for the onions

Ingredients:

- 3 cups (375 g) rinsed and cooked Japanese short-grain white rice
- 2 Japanese or Persian cucumbers, seeded and chopped
- handful of chopped dill
- 1 avocado, cubed
- 6 oz. (170 g) shelled edamame, blanched
- 1 tablespoon Everything Bagel seasoning
- 1 lemon, quartered

For the pickled red onions:

- ½ small red onion, thinly sliced
- 1 teaspoon honey
- 1 teaspoon salt
- ¼ cup (60 ml) rice, apple cider or white wine vinegar

For the slow roasted tomatoes:

- 12 oz. (340 g) fresh cherry or grape tomatoes
- Sprinkle of kosher salt
- Drizzle of olive oil

Instructions:

1. Preheat your oven to 300°F (150°C) degrees.
2. Place the sliced red onions in a bowl or jar with the honey, salt, and vinegar. Stir to combine and let sit for at least 30 minutes.
3. Slice cherry tomatoes in half, toss with olive oil and salt and place on 1–2 baking sheets. Roast for 75 minutes.
4. Serve a bed of rice in a bowl.
5. Place all ingredients artfully on top of the rice. I like to keep the ingredients separate for presentation.
6. Sprinkle dill and Everything Bagel Seasoning over the finished dish.
7. Serve with a wedge of lemon for some added acidity, if preferred.

Kristin Eriko Posner is a Japanese American who recently celebrated her bat mitzvah as an adult and is a student of Japanese tea ceremony. She is the founder of Nourish Co., an online resource of recipes and rituals for people and families of mixed ethnicities.

MIRIAM

STORY

Miriam is the daughter of Amram and Yocheved and the sister of Aaron and Moses. She is the first woman to be called a prophet. When she is young, she watches over her baby brother, Moses as he is placed in the Nile. When Pharaoh's daughter rescues Moses from the river, it is Miriam who convinces her to allow Yocheved to nurse him.

When the Israelites cross the Sea of Reeds to freedom, Miriam takes her tambourine and leads the women in dance. The Song of the Sea is attributed to her.

While in the wilderness, Miriam, along with Aaron, complain to Moses on behalf of Moses' wife. In all likelihood, the confrontation was a struggle over whose authority was to be recognized among the three siblings. As a result of challenging Moses' supreme authority, Miriam is afflicted with a skin disease and is separated from the camp for seven days. Nevertheless, Moses prays for her healing, and the community refuses to continue through the wilderness without their beloved Miriam.

Later tradition elaborates on Miriam's association with water. It is said, "As long as Miriam was alive, her well accompanied the Israelites through the desert. When she died, the well disappeared."

VERSES

"…she took a wicker ark for him and caulked it with resin and pitch and placed the child in it and placed it in the reeds in the banks of the Nile. And his sister stationed herself at a distance to see what would be done to him."

—Exodus 2:3–4

"And Miriam the prophetess, Aaron's sister, took the timbrel in her hand, and all the women went out after her with timbrels and dances. And Miriam sang out to them: "Sing to the LORD for he has surged, O surged, Horse and its rider He hurled in the sea!"

—Exodus 15:20–21

"And the Israelites, the whole community, came to the wilderness of Zin…and Miriam died there and was buried there. And the community had no water…"

—Numbers 20:1–2

THEMES

Leadership

Miriam is one of the few women in the Hebrew Bible who is designated as a prophet, not a fortune teller, but one who is a spokesperson for God. Unlike Moses, who is said to be slow of speech, Miriam has the courage to speak to the daughter of Pharaoh to save her brother. Nor is she afraid to confront Moses. She models both strength and divine compassion. She is part of the powerful triumvirate of Moses, Aaron and Miriam, who are instrumental in helping to lead the people of Israel out of bondage.

Hope through Music and Dance

Miriam plays a powerful role after the crossing of the Sea of Reeds. The Israelites have every reason to despair. Behind them are the Egyptians in pursuit, and before them is the foreboding desert. It is at that moment that Miriam leads the women in song and dance. A composer and a charismatic leader, she offers faith and hope for the future. In a time of peril, she teaches her community how to celebrate and sing.

In recent times, families include a cup for Miriam at the Passover Seder. Miriam's cup is filled with water and shared with all the Seder participants. As the wine in Elijah's cup holds the promise of redemption, the water in Miriam's cup sustains us on our journey to redemption and gives us hope.

MIDRASH

> The ancient rabbis ask: *"Whence did the Israelites have timbrels for dancing in the wilderness? Rather, the righteous trusted in God, they knew that He would perform miracles and mighty acts when they would go forth from Egypt, and they prepared for themselves timbrels and dancing".*
> —*Mekhilta de-Rabbi Ishmael*

After the people of Israel left Egypt, crossed the sea, it was Miriam who danced. Why? There were all those years of oppression, slavery, and nothing going right. She's the older sister, but her brother Moses gets all the acclaim. Moses gave us the Torah, tradition says, and the words echo through the generations to our own. But what about the Torah Miriam gave us?

Miriam danced. And I wonder, why? Caught between the sea, nature's fury, and the Egyptian army, human rage, it took an act of faith – or was it foolishness – to walk through the waters.

But what about all the mud and weeds, the women in long skirts carrying babies and everyone wearing the wrong shoes? Miriam's sandals couldn't have survived the crossing. I imagine she discarded them along with any excess baggage. She only kept the tambourine. What use could she have imagined for a musical instrument in the desert? Better a jug of water, I think.

And still Miriam danced. And I wonder why? She had to have questioned God. Why allow so many years of slavery? Why wait 400 years to hear the outcry of oppression. Really, what took so long? Why harden Pharaoh's heart, kill the Egyptian first born? She couldn't have believed that. She couldn't have thought that it was God who ordained it all and still sung praises.

And yet Miriam danced. Instead, she might have complained about the difficulties, despaired about the unknown tomorrow. Many who made the Exodus journey did just that.

She could have believed that music and dance were frivolous, an unnecessary distraction at such a serious and dangerous time. Yet Miriam lifted her tambourine and she made a sound, the sound of hope. And the people heard it carried in the wind, singing in the waves.

God hadn't sealed Pharaoh's heart; Pharaoh closed it himself. A large part of the miracle at the sea was the singing and dancing that Miriam led. There were other sea crossings, like Joshua across the Jordan, but no one sang and no one remembered. It was a wise choice Miriam made to carry on her freedom journey – the tambourine! Miriam danced and all the people joined her.

PROMPTS

Think of a time when someone made the sound of hope for you.

When have you wished you had had the courage to speak to someone in authority? Imagine doing it now. To whom would you speak and what would you say?

Reflect on something that others have considered inconsequential, even frivolous, that enabled you to move forward in your life.

Miriam's well sustained the Israelites in the wilderness. What and/or who sustains you?

Rabbi Sandy Eisenberg Sasso is the first woman to have been ordained a Rabbi in Reconstructionist Judaism. She is the Rabbi Emerita at Congregation Beth-El Zedeck in Indiana and the Director of Religion, Spirituality and the Arts, IUPUI Arts and Humanities Institute. She is the author of several nationally acclaimed children's books including: The Story of And: The Little Word that Changed the World, When God Gave Us Words, But God Remembered, Stories of Women from Creation to the Promised Land, and Noah's Wife; The Story of Na'amah.

GALETTE WITH PESTO, SUMMER SQUASH, AND CHERRY TOMATOES

Miriam's well, her guardianship over her young brother as he floated down the Nile River, and her leadership in song and dance on the shores of the Sea of Reeds all give water a central place in our understanding of Miriam's character. In this recipe, water gives life and form to the dough of the galette helping it to hold together to embrace the fillings within. However, too much water retained in the squash would weaken the dough. Balancing the water in this recipe, as Miriam brought balance to her family and community through navigating the tides of her time, is essential to creating a beautiful, whole, delicious galette.

While this recipe is a labor of love, what with the making of the dough, the squash filling, and the pesto – once you dig into the scrumptious galette, all of the hard work will be worth it. The whole-wheat flour gives the galette a good dose of fiber and a nutty taste that pairs nicely with the fresh herbs from the pesto.

Prep time: 30 minutes
Cook time: 70 minutes
Serves: 4–8 (4 as a main dish, 8 as a side dish)

Tools:

- Food processor
- 2 Sheet pans with silicone liners or parchment paper
- Large mixing bowl
- Rolling pin
- Measuring cups
- Measuring spoons

Ingredients:

- 1 zucchini, sliced into ¼ inch (6 mm) discs
- 1 yellow summer squash, sliced into ¼ inch (6 mm) discs
- 2 cups cherry tomatoes
- Up to 2 tablespoons extra virgin olive oil
- Salt and pepper
- Up to 4 heaping tablespoons vegan pesto (see below)
- 1 vegan galette dough (see below)
- Up to ¼ cup (30 g) whole wheat pastry flour for rolling out dough

For the vegan pesto:
- 1 bunch basil
- 1 bunch spinach
- 2 large garlic cloves, peeled and roughly chopped
- Juice of 1 small lemon

(continue on next page)

- ⅓ cup (45 g) pine nuts – for a nut-free version, substitute the same amount of roasted sunflower seeds
- ¾ teaspoon kosher salt
- Up to ¼ cup (60 ml) extra virgin olive oil

For the vegan galette dough:
- 1 ½ cups (180 g) whole wheat pastry flour (can substitute unbleached all-purpose flour)
- ½ teaspoon granulated sugar
- ¼ teaspoon kosher salt
- Optional: ½ teaspoon coarsely ground black pepper
- 6 tablespoons coconut oil or vegetable shortening (solid state), chilled and solid
- Up to 5 tablespoons ice water

Instructions:

1. Preheat your oven to 400°F (200°C).
2. Combine zucchini, squash, and cherry tomatoes in a large mixing bowl and season with salt and pepper to taste.
3. Drizzle the vegetables with 1 tablespoon olive oil and toss to coat the vegetables in the oil. Gradually drizzle in additional extra virgin olive oil, if needed. Arrange vegetables on a sheet pan lined with a silicone liner or parchment paper in one layer.
4. Bake in the oven for 10-15 minutes or until the vegetables have softened and shrunk but not browned. Remove from oven and cool completely.
5. While the vegetables are roasting, work on the galette dough. In a food processor, pulse together the flour, salt, and sugar (and black pepper, if using) a few times. Gradually add the chilled, solid coconut oil or vegetable shortening to the flour mixture in a food processor, pulsing until mixture resembles coarse meal.
6. Gradually drizzle in ice water until a dough just begins to come together, but is not wet or sticky. You will see balls of dough forming and catching in the food processor.
7. Remove the lid and blade from the bowl of the food processor and, using your hands, press the dough together into a ball.
8. Turn the dough out onto a clean, lightly-floured surface and press into a 7 inch (18 cm) disk with your fingers.
9. Transfer the dough disk to your silicone liner or parchment paper, floured side down, and use a lightly floured rolling pin to roll into a 14 inch (36 cm) circle.

10. Lift the silicone liner or parchment paper onto your baking sheet and chill in the refrigerator until 10 minutes before assembling your galette.

11. While the dough is chilling, work on the pesto. Combine the basil, spinach, garlic, lemon juice, pine nuts (or roasted sunflower seeds), and salt in the bowl of the food processor and pulse to combine.

12. Gradually drizzle in olive oil until the pesto comes together and appears creamy. Use immediately or store for future use: 5–7 days in the refrigerator, 3–4 months in the freezer.

13. To assemble the galette, make sure that the galette dough is pliable and your vegetables are cool. Work directly on the galette dough, on the lined sheet pan.

14. One spoonful at a time, spread up to 2 heaping tablespoons of pesto, starting in the center of your galette and working outwards leaving a 2–3 inch (5–8 cm) border, creating a generous layer of pesto in the center of your dough.

15. Maintaining the border, layer on half of the squash, zucchini, and tomatoes in a circular pattern on top of the pesto. Add small dollops and gently spread an additional 1–2 tablespoons of pesto on top of the layer of vegetables.

16. Arrange the rest of the vegetables in a circular pattern as the final layer in the center of your galette dough. It is worth taking the time to make this layer look nice as you will see it when the galette is finished.

17. Gently use both hands to gradually lift the edges of the galette dough and fold them in towards the center of the galette over the edges of the vegetable and pesto layers gently pressing to keep in place. This will create a 1–2 inch (3–5 cm) crust around the outside of your galette leaving much of the inside filling still visible. Do not worry if the dough cracks, gently seal the dough together or take a small piece from another edge to cover a hole and continue.

18. Bake the galette in the oven until lightly golden brown, around 40–50 minutes. Allow to cool before serving. Baking on the tray liner or parchment paper should allow for an easier transition to a serving platter, if you are using one.

19. Serve the galette warm or at room temperature. Use a sharp knife to slice into 4–8 even wedges.

Rabbi Jade Sank Ross grew up in Kinnelon, New Jersey. She graduated from Brandeis University with a Bachelor's Degree in Anthropology and International and Global Studies. She received her Master's Degree in Hebrew Literature and her Rabbinic Ordination from the Hebrew Union College – Jewish Institute of Religion. Currently, Jade serves as the Assistant Rabbi and Director of Education at Congregation Emanu-El of Westchester. As a food lover, Jade spends much of her free time in the kitchen cooking and baking. Jade and her husband, Rabbi Dan Ross, love to eat their way through their travels, visiting with family, and spend time with their dog Rashi.

TRIPLE-ALMOND BISCOCHOS

One of the most beautiful images associated with the prophetess Miriam is of her leading a group of women in celebratory song and dance by the Sea of Reeds. To honor her leadership and creativity I created an almond-centric adaptation of biscochos, a cookie beloved within the Sephardic community. The cookies' festive ring shape evokes Miriam's tambourine, and makes a sweet, naturally gluten-free treat. They are crisp and chewy, decadent and healthy, vegan and gluten free.

Prep time: 20 minutes
Cook time: 15 minutes
Serves: 20 (makes about 40 cookies)

Tools:

- Stand mixer fitted with a paddle
- Rubber spatula
- 2 large, rimmed baking sheets
- Parchment paper
- Measuring spoons
- Measuring cups
- 1 small bowl

Ingredients:

- 1 tablespoon chia seeds
- 3 tablespoons warm water
- 1 lb (454 g) almond paste
- 1 ¼ cups (150 g) almond flour
- 2/3 cup (130 g) plus 1/3 cup (65 g) granulated sugar
- ½ teaspoon almond extract
- ¼ teaspoon kosher salt
- 1 ½ teaspoons ground cinnamon

Instructions:

---

1. Grind the chia seeds in a spice grinder or coffee grinder until powdery and add to a small bowl. Stir in the warm water and let mixture sit until it gels, about 5 minutes.

2. Preheat the oven to 375°F (190°C) degrees and line two large, rimmed baking sheets with parchment paper.

3. Break up the almond paste into small pieces with your fingers and add to the bowl of a stand mixer fitted with a paddle attachment.

4. Add the almond flour, ⅔ cup sugar, almond extract, salt, and the chia mixture to the stand mixer and beat at low speed until a smooth, pliable dough forms. If the dough seems too dry or isn't coming together, beat in 1 additional teaspoon of water.

5. With slightly moist hands, pinch off a walnut-sized piece of dough and roll it into a 6-inch (15 cm) long rope, about ½-inch (12 mm) thick. Repeat with several more pieces of dough.

6. Use the tip of a small, sharp knife to score little slashes along the length of one side of the ropes, about ¼-inch (6 mm) apart.

7. Form each rope into a ring, gently pressing the ends together to seal and place on the prepared baking sheets. Repeat the process until all of the dough is used.

8. In a small bowl, stir the remaining ⅓ cup sugar with the cinnamon and lightly sprinkle the tops of the cookies with the cinnamon-sugar mixture.

9. Bake, rotating baking sheets once halfway through, until pale golden, 11–13 minutes. (Err on the side of less baked so the cookies remain chewy as they cool.)

10. Remove from oven and carefully transfer cookies to wire racks to cool.

Leah Koenig is a food writer and cookbook author. Her writing has been featured in The New York Times, The Wall Street Journal, Epicurious, Food52, Rachael Ray Everyday, Departures, and Tablet Magazine. Her cookbooks include Modern Jewish Cooking: Recipes & Customs for Today's Kitchen and Little Book of Jewish Feasts. Her latest project The Jewish Cookbook is a 425-recipe trove of traditional and contemporary Jewish recipes from around the world. Leah lives with her family in Brooklyn, New York and leads cooking demonstrations and classes worldwide.

RAHAB

STORY

Rahab, רחב, is a Canaanite harlot (*zona*) and innkeeper who lives in Jericho. She lives with her siblings and parents in a house built into the wall, on the border between the city and the outlying region. Her home reflects her vulnerable, marginal social status as a harlot. When Joshua sends two Israelite spies to Jericho, they stay at Rahab's inn. She protects them from the Canaanites by hiding them under flax on top of her roof and diverting their pursuers.

In a powerful speech, Rahab reveals her awe for YHVH. She knows of God's miracles, like the splitting of the sea, and she has heard that the other Canaanites are afraid of God's destructive power. Rahab foretells that the Israelites will conquer Jericho and she makes a deal with the spies to protect her and her family in exchange for assisting them. At the spies' instruction, Rahab ties a red string to her window and remains in her home during the ensuing battle. When Joshua and his troops come to conquer the city, they uphold the agreement and spare Rahab and her family, who live out the rest of their lives among the Israelites.

Like Yitro and Ruth, Rahab becomes a symbol of the righteous convert: an outsider who accepts YHVH as the one true God. It is said that she married Joshua and that kohanim (priests) and prophets descended from her.

VERSES

"And Joshua son of Nun sent out in secret two men as spies from Shittim, saying, "Go, see the land and Jericho." And they went and came to the house of a whore-woman whose name was Rahab, and they slept there."

—Joshua 2:1

"And now, pray, vow to me by the LORD, for I have done kindness with you, that you, too, shall do kindness with my father's house and give me a faithful sign, and let my father and mother live, and my brothers and sisters, and all that is theirs, and save our lives from death."

—Joshua 2:12–13

"And the town and all that is within it shall be under the ban to the LORD, except that Rahab the whore shall live and whoever is with her in the house, for she hid the messengers whom we sent."

—Joshua 6:17

THEMES

Beauty

The midrash identifies Rahab as one of the four most beautiful women of the Hebrew Bible (the others are Esther, Abigail, and Sarah). It is said that one who says her name three times cannot help but lust after her (*BT Megillah* 15a). Where does this come from? The original text (Joshua) doesn't seem to indicate that Rahab is particularly beautiful, except that attractiveness may correlate with her profession. Today, we may wish to imagine Rahab as beautiful in both looks and boldness, in deeds and words.

Faith

Rahab displays an incredible faith in God and God's power, citing the miracles God has performed for the Israelites in her speech to the spies (Joshua 2:9–11). This faith gives her the strength to courageously assist the spies and mislead the Canaanite pursuers. The red cord she hangs on her window is a symbol of this faith, in some ways parallel to the lamb blood the Israelites painted across their doorsteps while the ten plagues ravaged Egypt. Just as then, the red sign protected the inhabitants from death and destruction.

Wisdom

In addition to courage and faith, Rahab possessed the wisdom and foresight to discern the path to save herself and her family from destruction. She cleverly hid the spies and diverted the Canaanites. She took initiative in masterminding the escape plan. Rahab reminds us that wisdom can often come from unexpected people (a prostitute) and places (a hole in the wall), as we learn from *Pirkei Avot*: "Who is wise? The one who learns from every person" (4:1).

MIDRASH

> [*Rahab said to God*] *Master of the Universe! I have sinned with three things* [*with my eye, my thigh, and my stomach*]. *By the merit of three things pardon me: the rope, the window, and the wall.*"
>
> —*Mekhilta de-Rabbi Ishmael, Masekhta de-Amalek, Yitro 1*

Rahab is referred to as a *zona*, which means harlot or prostitute and is used as a contemporary Hebrew slur for women usually translated as "whore." Rahab's story has often been reduced to one about a woman who redeems her "sexual transgressions" via conversion to Judaism. This simplistic trope of the "reformed prostitute" misleads or distracts from more relevant or important issues in Rahab's story.

The alleged prostitution can be seen as a device that shows us the dire circumstances of her life: born into a socially marginalized non-Israelite family, she managed an inn – a place of transgression – in the liminal space of the wall.

Rahab has a chance encounter with two Israelite spies. Through this relationship she reveals that she holds within her an awareness of the God of Israel. This gives her strength and motivation to help the Israelite spies and to save herself and her family at the same time.

Prostitution is less important than Rahab's cleverness and wisdom (*bina*), courage (*ometz lev*) and her faith (*emunah*).

PROMPTS

How does Rahab's story change how we might look at women and others in our society who are called "whores" or other degrading names?

What situations make women today resort to prostitution? How much personal choice is involved?

Who are the "Rahabs" in our society and community today, people who are overlooked because of their lower social status?

Shirah Kraus is a rabbinical student at Hebrew Union College – Jewish Institute of Religion. She received her first degree from Bryn Mawr College where she studied Religion, Gender and Sexuality Studies, and Arabic. She wrote a senior thesis exploring community organizing as a religious practice. Shirah founded the J Street U chapter at Bryn Mawr and eventually served on the national student board. She loves to teach and work at camp (URJ-GUCI) where she will return as the Director of Jewish Education this summer. Shirah grew up in Cincinnati, Ohio with her parents and three siblings. Some of her hobbies include playing guitar, ultimate frisbee, crocheting kippot, reading young adult novels, and playing with her ten-year-old sister, Eden.

FERMENTED BREAD AND DATE BEER

As an innkeeper, Rahab is likely to have prepared refreshments for clients of all kinds. This beer is based on an ancient recipe, and primarily uses ingredients readily-available and familiar in biblical times.

Fundamentally, this is a wheat-based beer. Wheat must first be plucked, separated, and ground down in order to create the stuff of life: bread – an object of delight, of physical satisfaction. As with the wheat, so with the prostitute: first she must be taken, broken apart, and then ground down for use – except hers is a constant attrition for a perpetual stream of consumers.

Naturally-fermented, low-alcohol beer is a source of energy, rejuvenation, and refreshment – all of which would have been valuable qualities to a woman in Rahab's position, and to the people passing through her establishment. Fermented beverages contain naturally-occurring probiotic content, have therapeutic qualities, and are also known as digestive aids.

Prep time: 5 days

Cook time: 15 minutes

Serves: Makes enough for one group of guests, or enough to keep in the fridge for a few weeks of occasional drinking

Tools:

- Large sieve
- Small sieve
- Nut-milk bag or muslin for draining
- 2 large bowls or jars
- Funnel
- Glass or plastic bottles with screw-caps or flip-tops with a total capacity of ~2 litres

Ingredients:

- 1 lb. (450 g) stale, dry sourdough bread, preferably rye
- 10 cups (2.5 l) water
- ¾ cup (150 g) sugar*
- 1 cup (130 g) dates (weighed after removing seeds) or raisins
- 1 lemon, cut into narrow slices
- Optional: 1 tablespoon sourdough starter (100% hydration)
- Optional: Cinnamon stick, cinnamon bark, allspice berries, cloves, additional dried fruit

* Any sugar or natural sweetener will work – white, brown, or cane sugar, or date syrup (silan). The sugars will metabolise into acids during the fermentation process, leaving a mild sweetness and low-sugar content.

Instructions:

1. Preheat your oven to 340°F (170°C) degrees. Spread bread slices on a baking tray and toast until dark, but not burnt. Flip the bread after 5 minutes for even browning, and then toast for a further 5 minutes, or until the bread becomes deep golden-brown.

2. Remove the toasted bread from the oven and place in a large heat-proof container (jar, bowl, or a deep saucepan).

3. Boil 4 cups (1 l) water, leave to cool slightly, then pour over bread. Then add an additional 4 cups (1 l) of room-temperature water. Leave to soak for a minimum of 8 hours, or overnight.

4. Line the large sieve with muslin cloth or a nut-milk bag and place over a large bowl or jar. Pour the bread and water mixture into the sieve and use the fabric to squeeze out as much liquid as possible into the bowl.

5. In a small saucepan, heat the remaining water with the sugar until the sugar dissolves. Leave to cool slightly, add the dates or raisins, and then pour this mixture into the bowl containing the strained bread water.

6. For a more reliable fizz, add the active sourdough starter to the mix at this stage.

7. Cover the bowl with muslin cloth or a tea towel, and leave to soak for a minimum of 8 hours, or overnight.

8. Line up your clean bottles and drop lemon slices into each one. If desired, add any spices at this stage. Line the small sieve with muslin as before, and place on top of the funnel to decant the liquid, distributing evenly between the bottles. Lining the sieve with muslin or a nut-milk bag results in a clearer final product, and reduces silt build-up.

9. Close the bottles tightly and leave to ferment for 3 days at room temperature. Open the bottles daily in order to check and release carbonation build-up. When the beer fizzes enthusiastically upon opening, transfer the bottles to the fridge. Fermentation will continue, but at a slower pace. The beer will initially become more alcoholic, and then gradually more sour.

10. Open with caution and drink.

Sophie Kaye was born and raised in New Zealand. Sophie made aliyah to Israel in 2002 and never regretted the decision. Sophie is the mother of two interesting and kind kids, a healthy sourdough starter, and a collection of scobys. Her kitchen is a source of joy and experimentation, and a lively breeding ground for various healthy bacteria.

INDIVIDUAL POTATO KUGEL MUFFINS

Inns are places where travelers stop to eat, drink and sleep. As an innkeeper, Rahab would have needed to prepare food for her guests.

These potato kugel muffins would have been a convenient recipe for Rahab to prepare. They can be served warm or at room temperature and would work equally well as part of a breakfast spread, as bar snacks, and for guests arriving late at night. Most importantly, guests can just serve themselves.

These potato kugel muffins are made with zucchini and sweet potato for color and flavor. They are packed with fiber and nutrients from the different vegetables.

Prep time: 40 minutes

Cook time: 1 hour

Serves: 12

Tools:

- Large colander
- 2 large mixing bowls
- Box grater or food processor with grating blade
- Mixing spoon
- Muffin pan (nonstick)
- Muffin liners
- Baking spray

Ingredients:

- 3 small yukon gold potatoes
- ½ medium zucchini
- 1 medium sweet potato or yam
- ½ yellow onion
- 2 cloves garlic, minced
- ½ teaspoon sea salt or black salt
- ¼ teaspoon nutmeg
- ½ cup (60 g) matzo meal or breadcrumbs
- 3 Ener-G Egg Replacer eggs (4 ½ teaspoons + 6 tablespoons water)

Instructions:

1. Preheat your oven to 350°F (180°C) degrees.
2. Coarsely grate the potatoes, zucchini, sweet potato, and onion into a large colander sitting inside a large mixing bowl. Set aside for about 20 minutes to allow the vegetables to drain some of their liquid.
3. In a separate large mixing bowl, combine the garlic, sea salt, nutmeg, matzo meal and the Ener-G Egg Replacer eggs.
4. Press the vegetables in the strainer to remove as much of the liquid as possible, then transfer into the bowl with the matzo meal and spices. Stir well.
5. Line the muffin pan with muffin liners and lightly spray each liner with some baking spray. Fill to the top with the kugel mixture, smoothing off the tops of each one.
6. Bake for 1 hour. Let the kugel muffins cool a bit to set before serving.

From the Jewish Food Hero Kitchen

DEBORAH

STORY

Deborah is the only female character in the Bible described as both a prophet and a judge. She ruled in Israel during the period before the monarchy, when charismatic leaders served as political, judicial and military leaders of the fledgling Israelite nation. During this time of political instability, Deborah brought order to the people of Israel as a wise judge, dispensing guidance from her perch under the Palm Tree of Deborah. She also commanded the military officer Barak to wage war against Sisera, the general of the imposing Canaanite army. Deborah brought victory and salvation through the power of her prophetic words. (Her name plays on the Hebrew for "she spoke," *dibberah*.) *Devorah* literally means "bee," and she served as queen mother bee who directed her troops to swarm against the enemies of Israel, assuring protection and prosperity for her hive.

VERSES

"And Deborah, a prophet-woman, wife of Lappidoth, she it was who judged Israel at that time."

—Judges 4:4

"And she would sit under the Palm of Deborah between Ramah and Beth El in the high country of Ephraim, and the Israelites would come up to her for judgement."

—Judges 4:5

"Unwalled cities ceased,
in Israel they ceased,
till you arose, Deborah,
till you arose, O Mother in Israel."

—Judges 5:7

THEMES

Maternal Protection

The Song of Deborah describes her as "a Mother in Israel." However, Deborah is not a typical biblical mother. She is not defined by her role in birthing and raising children. In fact, the Hebrew Bible does not mention whether she has any children at all. In what ways is Deborah a "Mother in Israel?" She is the advisor who adjudicates the quarrels and quandaries of a disorganized society, bringing order to chaos. She is also the protector, who sees the threats to her people and who takes proactive risks with fierce determination to safeguard the future well-being of her nation.

Divine Victory

The character of Deborah highlights the biblical motif of women warriors. Deborah warns her army general, Barak, that if he insists that she accompany him into battle, the victory would come through "the hands of a woman." When women become unlikely heroines in the biblical narrative (like Esther, Deborah, and Yael), the Hebrew Bible is signaling that true salvation comes from the hand of God. It is not through bravado or military prowess that Israel is redeemed time and again. Deborah's prophetic voice and uncommon role reminds the biblical reader that "even a woman" can go to battle against an army of ten thousand and prevail, because it is ultimately God who brings about salvation.

MIDRASH

It was said about Deborah, "Deborah, wife (woman) of Lappidot, was a prophetess. What is meant by woman of Lappidot? That she made torches for the temple."

—Megillah 14a

The Hebrew Bible states, "Deborah, wife of Lappidot [*eshet lapidot*], was a prophetess." The rabbis of the Talmud derive "*eshet lapidot*" from the word *lapid* (torch). They understand Deborah's appellation as describing a woman who embodied special qualities (rather than ascribing her to a husband), much like Proverbs 31 describes the "*eshet hayyil*" ("Woman of Valor").

Thus, Deborah is "Woman of Torches" or "Woman of Flames." She lights the way for the Israelite people during a dark time. Emma Lazarus's famous poem, "The New Colossus," inscribed on the pedestal of the Statue of Liberty, invokes the character of Deborah. Lazarus writes, "A mighty woman with a torch, whose flame; is the imprisoned lightning, and her name; Mother of Exiles." Deborah was a "woman of torches" who was a "Mother in Israel." She stands out in the Hebrew Bible as a solitary, exceptional figure who embodies every form of human leadership and power: spiritual, intellectual, political and military. Just as the Statue of Liberty is intended to serve as a beacon of hope for people seeking refuge, Deborah brought hope and courage to her beleaguered nation and led the way to safety and victory.

PROMPTS

Deborah is described as a "mother," but not in relation to biological children. What are the characteristics and roles of a "mother" that can apply to any woman, regardless of whether she is a parent to children? In what ways do you act as "mother" in your life?

What kind of advice or guidance do people seek from you? Deborah sat under a palm tree to make herself available to her people. How do you make yourself available to others?

What tools do you use to battle the forces of darkness in the world? How are you holding up light in the world?

Rabbi Lauren Berkun is the Director of Rabbinic Programs for the Shalom Hartman Institute of North America. She graduated from Princeton University with a B.A. in Religion and was ordained at the Jewish Theological Seminary in 2001. Rabbi Berkun was a Wexner Graduate Fellow, a CLAL Rabbinic Intern, and a Rabbinic Fellow in the Shalom Hartman Institute Rabbinic Leadership Initiative. She has written and taught extensively on the topics of mikveh, sexual ethics, and body image. She is also a certified Sivananda yoga instructor.

MUSHROOM AND WALNUT GARDENER'S PIE
WITH BUTTERNUT SQUASH TOPPING

As a judge, Deborah must protect and enforce the rule of law. Justice is associated with the visual symbol of the scales, which represent the judge's role to weigh evidence.

At the same time, Deborah's name literally means "bee," an insect which plays a crucial role in maintaining ecological balance.

Without a fair judge, no justice. Without bees, no pollination and no crops.

To honor Deborah, the bee and the fragile balance of both justice and the natural environment, I offer this scrumptious gardener's pie filled with a bounty of fall vegetables. It is a hearty pie filled with warm flavors and a ton of nutrients from the mushrooms, lentils, walnuts, butternut squash, and leeks. It is also delicious with a plain potato topping.

Prep time: 15 minutes

Cook time: 90 minutes

Serves: 6–8

Ingredients:

- 1 small butternut squash, sliced lengthwise and deseeded
- 3 tablespoons olive oil, divided
- 2 medium leeks, thinly sliced
- 3 medium carrots, chopped
- 1 lb. (450 g) mushrooms, chopped
- 1 red chili pepper, deseeded and finely chopped
- 2 garlic cloves, minced
- 1 teaspoon dried thyme
- 1 ½ tablespoons white miso paste
- 3 cups (225 g) cooked lentils
- ½ cup (125 ml) vegetable broth
- 2 tablespoons soy sauce or tamari
- 3 oz. (90 g) walnuts, chopped
- ½ cup (125 ml) unsweetened oat milk, warmed
- salt and pepper to taste

Tools:

- Good knife
- Large frying pan
- Measuring cups and spoons
- Baking sheet
- Parchment paper
- Medium mixing bowl
- Potato masher
- Large casserole pan

Instructions:

1. Preheat your oven to 400°F (200°C) degrees.
2. Line a rimmed baking sheet with a piece of parchment paper and lay the two butternut squash halves, cut-side-down, onto the baking sheet. Place the squash into the oven to roast until fork tender, around 30–40 minutes.
3. While the butternut squash is roasting, heat a tablespoon of olive oil in a large frying pan over medium heat. Add the leeks and carrots; season with a fat pinch of salt and pepper. Cook, stirring occasionally, until the veggies become slightly soft, around 3–4 minutes.
4. Add in the mushrooms and season with another small pinch of salt to draw out the water from the mushrooms. Cook, stirring occasionally, until most of the water from the mushrooms cooks down, around 5–7 minutes.
5. Add in the chili pepper, garlic, and thyme; cook for another minute or until the garlic becomes really fragrant.
6. Add in the miso, lentils, broth, soy sauce and walnuts; season with another pinch of salt and pepper. Let the mixture bubble away until everything is nicely warmed through and slightly thickened, around 6–8 minutes.
7. Once the butternut squash is fork-tender, discard the peel and transfer the warm flesh into a medium mixing bowl. Add in the remaining two tablespoons of olive oil and the warm oat milk; mash with a potato masher until a smooth puree forms.
8. Transfer the mushroom and lentil mixture into a large casserole pan and top with the butternut squash puree. Place in the oven to bake until the pie becomes bubbly around the edges and the puree topping turns lightly golden-brown around the edges, around 10–15 minutes.
9. Leave to cool for a few minutes before serving.

From the Jewish Food Hero Kitchen

DATE PECAN BALLS

In Psalm 92 the date palm is described as enduring, steadfast, and strong. It is said to bear fruit even in its old age. Like the date palm, Deborah was steadfast and strong. She brought wisdom and ongoing guidance to those who approached her. She was consistent and nourishing. This recipe is in honor of eternal nourishment, Deborah, and the delicious date!

These delicious little date balls are packed with nutrients, but also great for an energy boost and as a healthy dessert. My family loves these in the fall and we keep them in the fridge for several days as a healthy go-to treat. Try rolling them in cocoa, coconut, or cacao nibs!

Prep time: 20 minutes
Cook time: 15 minutes
Serves: 20

Tools:

- Large skillet or saute pan
- Wooden or silicone spatula
- Medium metal mixing bowl
- Plate or platter
- Parchment paper

Ingredients:

- 2 ½ cups (325 g) Medjool dates, pitted and chopped
- 1 tablespoon soy-free Earth Balance or coconut oil
- ¼ cup nut butter (65 g) – cashew, almond, or peanut
- ¼ teaspoon Himalayan pink salt
- 2 cups (200 g) toasted chopped pecans

Instructions:

1. Melt the coconut oil/earth balance in a medium skillet over low heat and add in the chopped dates and nut butter. Cook, stirring constantly, until the dates soften and start to break down and lose their shape. Continue cooking and stirring until the oil blends in with the date and nut butter and the mixture starts to form a ball-like dough.
2. Remove the skillet from the heat and set aside to cool slightly.
3. Once the date mixture has cooled down for about 10–15 minutes, stir in the chopped pecans.
4. Using wet hands, gently roll the dough into 1 ½-inch (4 cm) balls. Arrange the formed balls on a large platter and continue rolling until you use up all of the mixture.
5. Refrigerate the balls for up to a week.

Mitten Lowe lives in Boulder, Colorado, USA, and is a mother of two, a wife, and a committed community member. She is a healer and owner of Journey to Wellness. She provides one-to-one treatments and facilitates group retreats that offer natural treatments for modern pathologies such as adrenal fatigue, gut healing, and food toxification.

YAEL

STORY

Yael's story is told within the narrative of Deborah. She is first identified as the wife of Heber the Kenite, a descendant of Moses' father-in-law Jethro (using another of his names, Hobab).

Yael is introduced at the pinnacle of a battle. The Canaanite general Sisera, having fled the Israelite general Barak, arrives at Yael and Heber's tent on foot. Weak and tired, Sisera seeks security, seclusion, and solace. Yael welcomes him and hospitably caters to his needs, covering him with a blanket and surreptitiously providing him with wine instead of milk.

Sisera falls asleep, at which point Yael seizes the opportunity to kill him with the "weaponry" she has on hand. She reaches for a tent peg and, using a large mallet, smashes it into Sisera's temple, killing him instantly. Her actions fulfill the prophecy of Deborah, who told Barak when he balked at going into battle without her "in the hand of a woman Adonai will deliver Sisera."

VERSES

"And she [Deborah] said, "I will certainly go with you, but it will not be your glory on the way that you are going, for in the hands of a woman the LORD will deliver Sisera."

—Judges 4:8–9

"And Jael came out to meet Sisera and said to him, "Turn aside, my lord, turn aside to me, do not fear." And he turned aside to her, to the tent, and she covered him with a blanket. And he said to her, "Give me, pray, a bit of water to drink, for I am thirsty." And she opened the skin of milk and gave him to drink and covered him."

—Judges 4:18–19

"And Jael wife of Heber took the tent peg and put a mallet in her hand and came to him stealthily and drove the peg through his temple and it sunk into the grounds – as for him, he had been asleep, exhausted – and he died. And, look, Barak was pursuing Sisera, and Jael went out to meet him and said to him, "Come, that I may show you the man you seek." And he went inside, and, look, Sisera was fallen, dead, the peg in his temple."

—Judges 4:21–22

THEMES

Tenacity

Yael's actions allow the Israelites to persevere in a difficult scenario, by incapacitating the enemy general at the time when the army is most vulnerable, in a panic. She takes decisive action and does so authentically, with determination and nerve.

Self-assurance

Although her motives are never revealed, Yael's conviction in the rightness of her actions is clear. She confidently reveals Sisera's hiding place and ultimate demise to Barak.

Craftiness

Yael uses her surroundings to her advantage. This is her tent, her space, and she owns it. She understands the situation enough to take advantage to her own benefit (and ultimately to the benefit of all Israel), giving Sisera wine and heightening his already weakened and tired state and fulfilling the prophecy that Sisera will succumb to the hands of a woman.

MIDRASH

"Yael fulfilled what is written in the Torah: A man's article shall not be upon a woman.[1] Therefore, she put her hand to the tent pin[2] [rather than to a weapon, which is considered a man's article]."

—*Targum Yonatan* on *Shoftim*, 5:26

Like many other biblical characters, especially women, Yael's inner monologue is withheld. Yael's motives remain a mystery, apropos of many episodes in the *TaNaKh*. Why does she decide to kill Sisera? Does she realize a battle is brewing between his army and the Israelite army? Does she feel threatened by his presence in her tent? As a warrior, her weaponry are everyday objects. How does she decide to take action? Does she merely lay her hands on the first item she sees? How much

---

1. Deuteronomy 22:5.
2. Judges 5:26.

forethought or pondering does she engage in before performing the dastardly deed? Does she push herself despite some personal trepidation or does she act unabashedly and wholeheartedly?

The intriguing thing about Yael's story is just how much it leaves out. This openness of interpretation is mirrored in the presentation of Yael's story in the biblical text: told first in a narrative form in chapter four and then reiterated but altered in the song of chapter five.

This story of this battle with the Canaanites and Yael's pivotal role in the Israelite victory is read as the haftarah portion during the reading of the Torah portion Beshalach (in which the Israelites cross the Sea of Reeds and celebrate their freedom and the defeat of the Egyptians with song and dance). This positions her as the third member of an impressive triad of women within that Torah reading, flanked by Miriam and Deborah.

In the Midrash and the Talmud, Yael is considered by the sages as being equal in righteousness and therefore worthy of blessing like the matriarchs Sarah, Rebecca, Rachel, and Leah. Yael's status as a revered, esteemed, virtuous warrior and mother-figure in the textual tradition is solidified with her association with all of these proud, strong female biblical figures.

Yael's actions could have been either a visceral reaction to a perceived lack of safety and her impulsive need for self-preservation, or might have been a calculated response to a complex military situation. One thing is clear: by occupying her own space and using her own external and internal tools, Yael secures victory for the Israelites and endures as a formidable biblical icon.

PROMPTS

Yael uses her surroundings to help her. As the midrash mentions, she relies upon the familiar tools at her disposal, rather than instruments outside her realm of competency. What tools, tangible or otherwise, do you have at your disposal that you could use to achieve your aims?

Yael takes the situation into her own hands, in a form of almost vigilantism or civil disobedience. How do you work outside the box, either professionally or personally? What causes are worth fighting for, in your opinion?

Have you ever chosen to do something without understanding why, which turned out to be positive? How did you feel when you realized the outcome was beneficial to yourself or others?

Yael kills Sisera when he comes to her seeking sanctuary. When have you felt betrayed by someone from whom you sought aid and assistance? Does Yael's action in this story help you understand how or why the other person might have acted this way?

Rabbi Lillian Kowalski *was ordained in 2019 by Hebrew Union College –*
Jewish Institute of Religion in Los Angeles, CA. She holds MAs in Hebrew Letters
and Jewish Education. Her published work focuses on communication
and its impact upon interpersonal relationships, and the fusion of Jewish
texts with creative arts. She holds a BA from Brandeis University in Near
Eastern and Judaic Studies, Music, and Women's and Gender Studies. She is
currently serving as the Rabbi-Educator of Temple Israel in Tulsa, OK.

POWER SLAW

Yael uses commonplace tools to her benefit. Following this theme, this recipe uses commonplace vegetables and fruits to benefit our health: cabbage, green peas, and apple.

This easy no-mayo and oil-free creamy coleslaw is colorful, delicious, and healthy. The green peas add additional protein to this salad, while the tahini in the dressing adds creaminess and a nutty flavor. Serve as a side dish for lunch or dinner meals.

Prep time: 15 minutes
Cook time: assembly only
Serves: 4–6

Tools:

- Food processor
- Large salad bowl
- Small salad bowl

Ingredients:

- 3 cups (210 g) red cabbage, thinly sliced
- 3 cups (210 g) green cabbage, thinly sliced
- 1 cup (150 g) fresh green peas (or organic frozen green peas)
- 1 granny smith apple, cored and thinly sliced
- 4 scallions, white and green parts only, minced
- Fresh cilantro, to serve

For the dressing:
- ¼ cup (60 ml) water
- ¼ cup (60 ml) fresh lime/lemon juice
- 3 tablespoons tahini
- 2 garlic cloves
- 1 ¼ teaspoon salt
- 1 teaspoon natural sugar
- ¼ teaspoon pepper
- ¼ teaspoon chili powder

Instructions:

1. First, make the dressing. Add all ingredients for the dressing in a high-powered blender and blend until smooth and creamy. Set aside.
2. In a large salad bowl, combine the thinly sliced cabbage and apple. Add in the peas and chopped green onion. Toss all the vegetables together.
3. Pour the dressing over the salad and gently mix everything together.
4. Serve the salad cold or at room temperature, garnished with fresh cilantro.

From the Jewish Food Hero Kitchen

COCONUT LIME BLACK CHIP POPSICLES

My name is Yaël and I imagine the biblical Yael would love these popsicles as a refreshment in the gruesome dessert heat. This recipe is inspired by one of my favorite Cambodian desserts: a black bean coconut popsicle. The lime and coconut pair perfectly together to form a refreshing treat. I also added in some mini vegan chocolate chips for some crunch and richness.

Prep time: 6 hours

Cook time: assembly only

Serves: 6

Tools:

- Mixing spoon
- Small prep bowl
- Popsicle molds
- Tablespoon and teaspoon measuring cups

Ingredients:

- 3 tablespoons mini vegan chocolate chips or cooked black beans
- 1 13.5-oz. (380 g) can coconut cream
- 1 ½ cup (375 ml) rice milk
- 4 tablespoons fresh lime juice
- 4 tablespoons honey
- 1 teaspoon vanilla extract
- Pinch of salt
- 1 teaspoon powdered agar agar
- 2 tablespoons water

195

Instructions:

1. In a small bowl, combine the powdered agar agar with the water and mix until the agar agar starts to dissolve. Let the mixture rest for 10 minutes.
2. In a large mixing bowl, stir together the coconut milk, rice milk, honey, salt, and lime juice. Add in the agar agar mixture and stir to combine.
3. Pour the coconut lime mixture into popsicle molds filling them ¾ of the way. Add ½ tablespoon of chocolate chips or black beans to each popsicle mold.
4. Pour the remaining coconut milk mixture into the popsicle molds to top them off and place the freezer for 4–5 hours or overnight.

Yaël Alfond-Vincent is a French-American who was born in Switzerland in 2010. She grew up in Cambodia where she was a student at Ecole Française de Battambang. In her free time, Yaël loves to read and spend time with her friends.

HANNAH

STORY

Hannah was Elkanah's favorite wife. She was struggling to conceive a child and often felt alone, especially when Penina, Elkanah's other wife, reminded Hannah of her fertility issues. Elkanah was loyal to Hannah, and Hannah was loyal to God.

One night after a big meal, Hannah was particularly upset and went to the temple to pray. She wept to God. In her silent, personal prayer, she vowed that if she was blessed with a son, his life would be dedicated to serving God. It was then that she encountered Eli, the high priest, who mistook her tears and silent muttering for drunkenness. When Hannah explained that she wasn't drunk but upset, Eli offered Hannah a blessing. God remembered Hannah and her prayers, and she conceived a child soon afterward.

Hannah named her son Samuel which means "I asked God for him". Staying true to her vow, Hannah did not go with her family to make the annual sacrifice that year, waiting to return to the temple when Samuel was a little older. When her son was ready, Hannah took him and a number of offerings to Eli and offered her son as a servant to God. Following her sacrifice, Hannah once again prayed to God, this time in praise. As Hannah left, Eli blessed her by asking God to grant Hannah more children. God responded, and Hannah lived in blessing with three more sons and two daughters.

VERSES

"And she vowed a vow and said, "LORD of Armies, if you will really look on Your servant's woe and remember me, and forget not Your servant and give Your servant male seed, I will give him to the LORD all the days of his life, no razor shall touch his head."

—1 Samuel 1:11

"…as Hannah was speaking in her heart, her lips alone moving and her voice not heard, Eli thought she was drunk."

—1 Samuel 1:13

But Hannah did not go up, for she had said to her husband, "Till the lad is weaned! Then I will bring him and we will see the LORD's presence, and he shall stay there always."

—1 Samuel 1:22

THEMES

Loyalty

Hannah prays to God in a moment of intense sadness and vows her future son's service to God if her prayers are answered. When God blesses her with a son, Hannah remains true to her vow and praises God again. Hannah does not forget her vow to God once she is out of a state of despair.

Independence

Hannah's fate changes when she approaches God with her prayers. During her time, people attempted to connect with God through offerings rather than personal prayers. Hannah finds the words to ask God for what she needs and to communicate what she will offer in return. When questioned by Eli, Hannah is able to defend herself against his accusations and questions about why she is there alone, explaining that she is conversing with God. Hannah's choice to use her own words is perhaps a key reason that God and Eli both respond by bestowing blessings onto her.

MIDRASH

"R. Hamnuna said: *How many of the most important laws can be learnt from the verses relating to Hannah. Now Hannah, she spoke in her heart: from this we learn that one who prays must direct their heart. Only her lips moved: from this we learn that one who prays must frame the words distinctly with their lips. But her voice could not be heard: from this, we learn that it is forbidden to raise one's voice in the Tefillah. Eli thought she had been drunk: from this, we learn that a drunken person is forbidden to say the Tefillah.*"

—*Berakhot* 31a

When Eli saw Hannah, a woman coming to the House of God late at night distraught and alone, he was confused. He judged Hannah because her actions were unfamiliar. From their conversation, Hannah teaches Eli another way to connect with God.

Hannah's desperation for comfort could have made her vulnerable, but she used her pain to find inner determination and willingness to create a personal conversation with God. In sharing this with Eli, she changes his mind and he sees her inner strength. This new perspective transforms his initial judgement of her, and he offers a blessing to Hannah in return.

Hannah is often seen as the pioneer who brought personal prayer into Judaism. Our sages, including Rabbi Hamnuna, recognize this by establishing standards of prayer from Hannah. From Hannah we learn that personal prayer must be intentional and come from the heart.

PROMPTS

What drives you to pray?

Hannah's prayer to God includes a vow that she keeps. Think of a time when your prayers included a vow to God. Did you keep your vow? Why or why not?

Hannah's personal prayer sets the precedent that prayers must come from the heart. When do you pray from your head? How does the experience, and perhaps what you request, differ when you pray from your heart?

Elana Rabishaw is a Rabbinic and Education student at Hebrew Union College- Jewish Institute of Religion in Los Angeles, California. Born and raised in California, Elana is happy to study on the Los Angeles campus after graduating from the University of Wisconsin- Madison (Go Badgers!). If graduate students had free time, Elana would enjoy going to the ocean, watching all of the Chicago sports games, and baking anything with chocolate.

VEGAN POTATO AND SPINACH PATTIES

I like to think of Hannah visiting Samuel at the temple often, showering him with hugs, kisses, and packages of home cooked food. These vegan and spinach patties would have been a perfect choice for a satiating, portable food as they can be eaten warm or cold, eaten with a fork or just with our hands.

My maternal grandmother used to make these from day-old mashed potatoes. Her recipe included milk, eggs, and butter. I wanted a healthier potato and spinach patty, so I've adapted my grandmother's traditional recipe with healthy ingredients that are all plant-based.

Prep time: 15 minutes

Cook time: 1 hour

Serves: 8, makes 12–14 patties

Tools:

- Large soup pot
- Good knife
- Cutting board
- Prep bowl
- Potato masher
- 2 non-stick baking trays
- Spatula

Ingredients:

- 3.5 lbs. (1.6 kg) potatoes, peeled and diced small
- 1 large onion, diced small
- 3 cups (750 ml) good water (you do not drain it, this water stays in the recipe)
- 2 cups (60 g) raw spinach, chopped
- ½ teaspoon salt
- ⅛ teaspoon pepper
- 1 cup (125 g) breadcrumbs

Instructions:

1. Place potatoes, onion, water, salt, and pepper into a large soup pot over medium heat and simmer until potatoes are well-done and mushy and the water is absorbed, approximately 30 min. Make sure the bottom does not burn as the water absorbs.
2. Remove from heat and use a potato masher to mash everything together until smooth and lump-free. Stir in the chopped spinach and taste. Adjust the seasoning to taste.
3. Preheat your oven to 400°F (200°C) degrees.
4. Form the potato mixture into patties – you should get around 12–14 patties in total.
5. Lightly coat each patty in breadcrumbs on all sides and gently place on a non-stick baking tray. Repeat with all patties.
6. Bake until slightly golden-brown and crispy, around 20 minutes, flipping halfway through.
7. Serve hot or cold with ketchup, mustard, pickle relish, or any condiment of your choice.

From the Jewish Food Hero Kitchen

GLUTEN-FREE GINGER MOLASSES COOKIES

One of the ideas presented in Hannah's story is that God remembered her. Of course it is not the same type of "remembering," but the idea made me think about how parents remember and try to cater to their children's food preferences. Most children (and adults) enjoy cookies. As parents, we can create healthier versions of cookies which meet a balance point between what our kids want and what we think is best for them.

I was thinking of Hannah as a mother when I found David Lebovitz's nonfat molasses cookie recipe. His recipe was made with natural sugar and real spices – healthy versions of the usual cookie ingredients. The complex adult flavours offer an alternative to the cliché sweets and treats kids are usually offered.

This recipe is inspired by Lebovitz's recipe, in particular his use of black pepper. This version is vegan and includes aquafaba as an effective and magical egg replacer. It is also gluten-free, includes grated fresh ginger and less sugar.

Prep time: 20 minutes
Cook time: 15 minutes
Serves: 12

Tools:

- Mixing bowl
- Electric mixer (whisk attachment)
- Measuring cups and spoons
- Cookie sheet pan
- Ice cream scoop

Ingredients:

- ½ cup (90 g) dark or light brown sugar
- ¼ cup (75 g) applesauce
- 1/3 cup (100 g) molasses, blackstrap or mild-flavoured
- 1 ¾ cups (250 g) gluten-free oat flour
- ½ cup (65 g) brown rice flour (white rice flour or all-purpose GF flour would also work)
- 1 teaspoon baking soda
- 2 ½ teaspoons ground cinnamon
- 1 ½ teaspoons ground ginger
- ¼ teaspoon ground cloves
- ½ teaspoon freshly-ground black pepper
- ¼ teaspoon salt
- Zest of 1 lemon
- 1 tablespoon vanilla extract
- 4 tablespoons aquafaba (the liquid from a can of chickpeas)
- 3 tablespoons fresh ginger, grated
- Additional sugar and cinnamon for dusting, optional

Instructions:

1. Preheat oven to 350°F (170°C) degrees.
2. In the bowl of an electric mixer, add the brown sugar, applesauce, and molasses. Beat with the whisk attachment until light and fluffy, around 5 minutes.
3. In a separate bowl, whisk both flours, baking soda, ground cinnamon, ground ginger, ground cloves, black pepper, and salt. Set aside.
4. Add the zest of 1 lemon, vanilla extract, aquafaba, and freshly grated ginger to the bowl of wet ingredients.
5. With the mixer running on low speed, slowly add the dry ingredients into the wet. Beat until combined and a soft batter forms.
6. Set aside and let the mixture thicken slightly, around 10 minutes.
7. Using an ice cream scoop, scoop portions of the thickened batter and place on large sheet pan lined with parchment paper.
8. Bake until the cookies turn light golden-brown and slightly puffy, around 12–15 minutes.
9. Let the cookies cool completely before dusting with cinnamon and sugar, if using.

From the Jewish Food Hero Kitchen

ABIGAIL

STORY

Abigail was married to an emotionally abusive man named Nabal who disrespected the future king David by refusing to provide rations for his entourage.

When David arrived with his army to decimate Nabal's entire household, Abigail stealthily went out to meet him. She expressed her belief that he would be the next King of Israel and persuaded him that when that happened he would not want it known that he had spilled blood freely. As an alternative, she offered him an abundance of rations from Nabal's property. David was convinced and turned away, after blessing Abigail for saving him from himself. When Abigail told Nabal what had transpired, he became ill and died 10 days later.

David was so impressed with Abigail's wisdom, that after Nabal's death he requested her hand in marriage and she agreed immediately, becoming his third wife.

VERSES

"And Abigail hurried and fetched two hundred loaves of bread and two jugs of wine and five dressed sheep and five seals of parched grain and a hundred raisin cakes and two hundred fig cakes…"

—1 Samuel 25:18

"And so, when the LORD does for my lord all the good that He has spoken about you and He appoints you prince over Israel…you will remember your servant."

—1 Samuel 25:30–31

"And David's servants came to Abigail at Carmel and spoke to her, saying, "David sent us to take you to him as a wife…and she went after David's messengers and she became his wife."

—1 Samuel 25:40–42

THEMES

Wisdom

Despite her desperate situation, Abigail didn't wait for tragedy to befall her household. She cleverly evaded Nabal to speak to David and bring him what he had asked for. She understood that David's honor had been tarnished, so she went about restoring it, expressing her belief in his innate goodness and shining future.

Optimism

Although Abigail was trapped in an unhappy marriage, she knew that most people were essentially good, and she appealed to David's good nature to save her household. She recognized that her actions could elevate her circumstances, so she acted even though the odds were stacked against her. After her husband's death, she didn't give up on the institution of marriage and instead accepted David's proposal.

MIDRASH

"Abigail was better for David than all the sacrifices in the world, for if David had carried out the murder of Nabal, all the sacrifices in the world would not have sufficed to atone for his sin, and she came and saved him from it."

—*Midrash Shochar Tov*, Psalm 53

Abigail is almost entirely absent from the biblical story after her marriage to David. We know that she was captured by the Philistines and released by David, and that she settled with him in Hebron, where she gave birth to his son, Cileab.

The midrash above hints at the relationship between Abigail and David. David was an impetuous man, prone to emotional decisions, and Abigail was the sensible and logical one. She balanced him out as best she could and likely prevented him from many unwise decisions (although he still made a number of famous mistakes).

Some of David's marriages were essentially political alliances, but his relationship with Abigail was clearly based on mutual respect and possibly even love. One imagines that she supported him during his long and challenging ascent to the throne and that he loved and appreciated her for it.

Abigail is a symbol of strength, wisdom and optimism. She extricated herself from an abusive marriage and married a man who respected her and whom she could respect in turn.

PROMPTS

What are the characteristics which I look/looked for in a soulmate? What makes these characteristics so attractive?

How do I react in challenging situations? Do I wish that I reacted differently?

"It can always be worse." This isn't always simple to see when you're in a dire situation. If you're faced with a big challenge, write down three ways in which it could be worse, and three blessings you may be forgetting to appreciate.

Hadassah Levy is a digital marketer specializing in Jewish content who teaches and learns Torah as often as possible. She studied Talmud at Bar Ilan University and at Matan Women's Institute for Torah Study. She previously taught in seminaries and teaches classes in her community. She lives in Eli, Israel with her husband and 4 children.

SPELT SOURDOUGH LOAVES

Loaves of bread, among other things, were offered by Abigail to David, and many of them at that. It was a historical offering of peace by the righteous and wise Abigail. Although not specified in the scripture, spelt would have made for a healthy offering as well, and who knows...maybe it was.

Spelt is an ancient grain from the wheat family. It can reduce the risk of diabetes, and is good for digestion among many other health benefits. This spelt sourdough loaf is tasty and nutritious, great for sandwiches, and keeps well.

Prep time: 10 hours
Cook time: 30 minutes
Serves: 2 loaves

Tools:

- Scale
- Medium mixing bowl or stand mixer
- Small bowl
- Bench knife
- Two proofing baskets or two sieves and tea towels
- Baking stone/baking steel

Ingredients:

- ¾ cup (200 g) active sourdough starter
- 3 ½ (500 g) whole spelt flour
- 4 cups (500 g) white spelt flour
- 3 cups (750 ml) cold water
- 1 tablespoon + 1 teaspoon salt
- 2 ½ cups (200 g) spelt flakes

Instructions

1. In a large mixing bowl, combine 2 ¾ cups (700 ml) water with the sourdough starter. Add in the spelt flour and mix well, making sure all of the flour is hydrated.

2. In a separate smaller bowl, dissolve the salt with the remaining water and add to the dough.

3. Using your hands or an electric mixer, knead the dough for 3–5 minutes. Cover with a plastic wrap and set aside to rise for 90 minutes. Every 30 minutes, fold the dough 3 times over. You will need to do this 3 times during the 90-minute interval.

4. After the last fold-over, cover the dough well and let it ferment in a cool place for 5–8 hours. The fermentation time will depend on how active your starter is and on the temperature of the dough.

5. Divide the dough into two parts. Shape round or oblong.

6. Preheat the oven with the baking stone/steel to 450°F (230°C) degrees.

7. Add the spelt flakes on a plate and fill a small bowl with some water. Dip the loaf into the water and then immediately put in on the plate with the spelt flakes, making sure the surface of the loaf is completely covered with the flakes.

8. Place the loaf into the proofing basket seam side up. Repeat with the second loaf. Leave the loaves to prove, covered, for about an hour.

9. Invert the loaves onto the baking paper and place them into the oven. Bake for 10 minutes with steam and for another 30 minutes without.

10. Remove from the oven and cool completely on a cooling rack.

Chana Schroff is a professional teacher by trade, self trained artisan baker and bread enthusiast. She has been baking breads and cakes for upwards of twenty years, and baking with sourdough for almost seven years. She emphasises the importance of baking with heritage grains and milling at home.

VEGAN RUM RAISIN TAPIOCA PUDDING

This recipe is a nod to Abigail's choice to share a hundred clusters of raisins with David.

Tapioca is made from cassava (yuca) – a root vegetable. It is considered kosher for Passover. Tapioca is an underappreciated, somewhat retro food which can be enjoyed by everyone, from babyhood to old age. It is gooey and creamy and eaten by the spoonful.

This tapioca pudding is perfect for breakfast or dessert because it is comforting, satiating and versatile. The added rum soaked raisins make the dessert fancy. You could switch the raisins for any other dried fruit or add fresh fruit at the end after cooking.

Prep time: 30 minutes
Cook time: 20 minutes
Serves: 4–6

Tools:

- Medium strainer
- Medium saucepan
- Individual bowls for serving

Ingredients:

- ½ cup (75 g) small tapioca pearls, rinsed under cold water and drained
- 3 ½ cups (875 ml) good mineral water
- ½ cup (125 ml) coconut milk cream
- ¼ cup (60 g) natural cane sugar
- 1 teaspoon vanilla extract
- ½ cup (75 g) raisins
- 2 tablespoons dark rum (or brandy)
- ¼ teaspoon kosher salt

Instructions:

1. In a small bowl, combine the raisins with the rum and set aside.
2. Place tapioca pearls in a medium saucepan and add 3 cups (750 ml) of water. Soak the tapioca for 30 minutes and don't drain the water after soaking.
3. Once the tapioca has been soaked, add in the coconut cream, sugar, rum-soaked raisins with any leftover rum, and kosher salt.
4. Place over medium heat and cook, stirring frequently, until mixture comes to a gentle boil. Then, reduce the heat to low and simmer, uncovered, stirring frequently, until mixture is thick, around 10–15 minutes. If the mixture becomes too thick, add a bit more water.
5. Divide the mixture into bowls and either serve immediately or cover so that the pudding does not develop a crust
6. Serve warm or chilled.
7. Optional: Garnish with berries.

From the Jewish Food Hero Kitchen

WOMAN OF SHUNEM

STORY

Though unnamed, the woman of Shunem is introduced in 2 Kings 4 as *isha g'dola*, meaning "great woman," "wealthy woman," or "woman of status."

Her story begins when the prophet Elisha is passing through Shunem and the local "great woman" insists he come in for a meal. Elisha then makes a habit of stopping in for a meal whenever he passes through. The Shunammite woman observes that Elisha is a man of God, and tells her husband that they should build a room in their house for his use whenever he passes through. Grateful for this act of hospitality, Elisha – through his servant Gehazi – asks the woman what he can do for her in return. She indicates that she is not in need. Elisha then asks his servant Gehazi what can be done for this woman, and Gehazi responds by saying that the woman has no son and her husband is old. Elisha tells the woman she will soon bear a son. She asks Elisha not to deceive her, and within a year she does indeed give birth to a son.

One day the child goes out to the threshing floor, suffers a head injury, and dies in his mother's lap. The Shunammite woman lays the child on Elisha's bed and rides off hastily to the prophet. Gehazi tries to prevent her from interacting with Elisha, but the woman throws herself at the prophet's feet and he recognizes her urgent need. "Did I ask my lord for a son?" she charges Elisha, "Didn't I say: 'Don't mislead me'?" The prophet gives his staff to Gehazi and sends him to revive the boy, but the Shunammite woman refuses to return without the prophet himself, so he accompanies her. Elisha brings the child back to life.

The Shunammite woman appears again in 2 Kings 8. At Elisha's behest, her family has been residing abroad for seven years to avoid famine. Returning, she seeks restoration of her house and lands from the king. She happens to walk in with her son when Gehazi is telling the monarch of the miracle Elisha performed when he brought a boy back from the dead. Seeing them walk in, Gehazi says, "this is the woman and this is her son whom Elisha revived." The king questions the Shunammite woman, and, after she tells him her story, he restores her property and orders that she be paid lost revenue.

VERSES

"And one day Elisha was passing through Shunem, and there was a wealthy woman there. And she urged him to break bread, and so, whenever he passed through, he would turn aside there to break bread."

—2 Kings 4:8

"And she said to her husband, "Look, pray, I know that he is a holy man of God who always passes by us. Let us make, pray, a little upper chamber and put a bed there for him and a table and chair and lamp, and so when he comes to us, he will turn aside there.""

—2 Kings 4:9–10

"And he said, "At this fixed time, at this very season, you will embrace a son." And she said, "Don't my lord, man of God, don't mislead your servant.""

—2 Kings 4:16

THEMES

Hospitality

Like Sarah, who shares a similar story of unexpected motherhood and who also nearly loses her son, the woman of Shunem exemplifies the Jewish pillar of hospitality. Elisha is a prophet, a man who owns little and relies on God to provide him with food and shelter. The Shunammite woman not only offers him a meal, she insists upon it, feeds him regularly whenever he passes through her town, and even goes so far as building and furnishing a room in her house for him. The woman of Shunem does this without expectation of reward, even turning down the prophet's offer of repayment and only asking something of him when her son's life is at stake.

The Role of Women in the Biblical Era

The Shunammite woman is a woman of contradictions, serving as both a typical and an atypical female biblical character. Although nameless (a feature common to biblical women), she is known in her own right rather than in relation to a man (as the wife or daughter of a male biblical character). Her husband is also nameless, but while he is known only as "old," she bears an epithet that indicates a high social status. She wields more power than most biblical women as master of her house, decision maker, and advocate, but she is characteristically conceived of as incomplete until she becomes the mother of a son. She communicates with and even influences the decisions of a prophet, but the prophet speaks to her only through his servant, referring to her not as a "great woman," but as "that Shunammite woman" in a tone that can be read as belittling, if not derogatory.

MIDRASH

"Once she said to her husband, 'I am sure it is a holy man of God who comes this way regularly'" (2 Kings 4:9). How does the Shunammite woman know that Elisha is holy? According to the Rabbis, she observes that Elisha refuses to look at her. Whoever guards himself against a married woman, the Rabbis decree, is holy.

—*Vayikra Rabbah*

The Rabbis imagine Elisha refusing to look at the Shunammite woman, elevating this act to something holy. A man guarding himself against a married woman may have been the convention at the time of the Rabbis, or they may have been attempting to instill in men a fear of women's power. By refusing to look at the great woman of Shunem, the prophet makes clear that she is to be guarded against because of her gender. The Shunammite woman is a remarkable character with much to teach us about graciousness and loving-kindness. What does Elisha fail to see by averting his eyes?

The Shunammite woman possesses uncharacteristic power and autonomy for a woman of biblical literature, serving as decision-maker for her household:

- she insists Elisha come in and eat;
- she decides a room should be built for him;
- she turns down his offer of repayment;
- she rides off to fetch him when her son dies;
- she ensures that the prophet himself comes to revive her son; and
- she appeals to the king for restoration of her family's lands.

So, too, is the woman of Shunem exemplary of hospitality, of *tzedakah*, of *chesed*. The Rabbis consider her one of twenty-three upright and righteous women (*Midrash Tadshe*) and an *Eshet Chayil*

("Woman of Valor"), applying to her the verse from Proverbs 31: "She gives generously to the poor; her hands are stretched out to the needy" (*Midrash Eshet Hayil*).

What were the Rabbis teaching when they celebrated Elisha's refusal to look at such a woman? Such rules may have been created in an attempt to protect marriage and fidelity, but they did not apply equally to men and women, and they have resulted in a longstanding fear of – and prejudice against – women.

The Torah is a living, breathing entity that has new lessons to teach every generation. Today, from the *TaNaKh* to the midrash, the story of the Shunammite woman highlights the importance of seeing women and of celebrating them for their accomplishments rather than reducing them to – and being fearful of – their gender.

May we all be like the woman of Shunem, serving our fellow humans in hospitality, kindness, and generosity. May we all see holiness in others. And may those who exemplify such righteousness be seen for all the ways they increase holiness in the world.

PROMPTS

Even after the Shunammite woman's audacious hospitality, Elisha refuses to speak to her directly. How have you been silenced, unseen, unheard, or otherwise marginalized because of your gender?

Elisha and Gehazi decide that the Shunammite woman needs a son. Although typically a gift (if not a necessity) in the biblical era, today this interaction would be more complicated. How does today's Jewish community view childlessness and childlessness-by-choice?

Reflect upon three of the Shunammite woman's key strengths. Which women in your own life model these traits?

Sivan Rotholz is a professor of feminist Torah and creative writing. She has taught at Brooklyn College and Tel Aviv University, facilitates private classes for artists and writers, and serves as a scholar-in-residence for various synagogues and writing residencies. Her work has appeared in the Jewish Journal, diode, Bearings, and Mayday Magazine, among other journals and anthologies. She is the Education Director for Achayot, America's first residency for Jewish women and non-gender conforming writers. Sivan earned her MFA in poetry from Brooklyn College in 2013 and is currently pursuing rabbinic ordination at Hebrew Union College – Jewish Institute of Religion.

VEGETABLE BROTH WITH KREPLACH

The Women of Shunem suffers the excruciating experience of her child's death. Her refusal and inability to accept that her son had died made me think of the Yom Kippur "gates of prayer" closing after the concluding Ne'ila prayer. As a parent, like the Woman of Shunem, it is impossible to conceive of the idea that the gates of prayer ever close when it comes to our children.

It is customary to eat kreplach dumplings served in a broth on the eve of Yom Kippur. By offering the Woman of Shunem this soup, I am connecting her story with the moment when the gates of prayer are still open.

Traditional Kreplach dumplings recipes include egg in the dough and a meat filling. This recipe includes a gluten-free dough and a satisfying mushroom, potato, and herb filling.

Prep time: 30 minutes

Cook time: 1 hour & 30 minutes

Serves: 6–8

Tools:

- Electric mixer with dough hook
- Food processor
- Soup pot
- Rolling pin
- Scale
- Measuring spoons
- Knife
- Strainer

Ingredients:

For the kreplach dough:
- ½ cup (70 g) rice flour
- 1 cup (130 gr) gluten free flour
- ½ cup (110 ml) water
- Pinch of salt
- For the kreplach filling:
- ½ lb. (250 g) mushrooms
- 1 cup (100 g) cooked, mashed potato
- 1 garlic clove
- 2 tablespoons fresh parsley, minced (or 1 tablespoon fresh thyme)
- 1 tablespoon scallions, diced
- 1 teaspoon salt
- ½ teaspoon pepper
- 1 tablespoon vegetable broth

For the vegetable broth:
- 6 cups (1,5 l) water
- 3 carrots
- 1 sweet onion
- 3 garlic cloves
- 2 celery stalks
- 1 sprig of thyme
- 4 whole peppercorns
- 1 tablespoons salt
- You can also use store-bought vegetable broth.

Instructions:

1. To make the vegetable broth, wash all vegetables (but don't peel them) and chop into rough chunks.

2. In a large soup pot, add all the vegetables and water; bring to a boil over medium-high heat. Reduce the heat to medium and simmer for 45 minutes.

3. Strain the mixture in a large heat-proof bowl. Compost the vegetables. Place the strained broth back in the pot and set aside.

4. Next, work on the dough. Add the rice flour, gluten-free flour, water, and a pinch of salt to the bowl of an electric mixer fitted with a dough hook and knead until a smooth dough forms, around 5–7 minutes.

5. Transfer the dough onto a lightly floured surface and using a rolling pin, roll out the dough into a thin rectangle. Cut out 2×2-inch (5×5 cm) squares from the dough and set aside.

6. To make the filling, saute the onion and garlic in a tablespoon of vegetable broth over medium heat. Add in the mushrooms and cook until they develop a bit of color and most of their water evaporates, around 7–8 minutes. Remove from heat.

7. In a food processor, combine the mushroom and onion mixture, mashed potato, scallions, and parsley; blitz a couple of times or until the mixture is just combined.

8. To assemble the kreplach, place a little bit of the filling on one side of the kreplach dough square and pull the other side over to cover the filling, creating a rectangle. To ensure the filling is tightly enclosed within the dough, press open side together with a floured fork.

9. Bring the vegetable broth to a simmer and gently drop each kreplach filled dough pocket into the broth. Simmer over medium heat for around 10–12 minutes.

10. Serve the kreplach in the vegetable broth and season with additional salt and pepper, if needed.

From the Jewish Food Hero Kitchen

MAPLE POACHED PEARS WITH CINNAMON AND CARDAMOM

My mother taught me to boil cinnamon sticks to make the house smell sweet and inviting. Even if the food is cooked the day before or the party isn't a sit-down meal, the scent of cinnamon cooking makes the house feel welcoming.

The Woman of Shunem was a gracious hostess and welcomed others into her home. Her hospitality inspired this dish that uses my mom's cinnamon trick. Making these delicious poached pears will make your house smell and taste like home to whoever may be passing through.

Perfectly sweet and spiced with cinnamon and cardamom, these poached pears will be a wonderful ending to any dinner. The maple syrup gives them a lovely caramel-like taste, while the tart lemon juice helps cut through the sweetness. Served with some velvety coconut cream or non-dairy yogurt, it's the perfect dessert that will please any guest at your dinner table.

Prep time: 10 minutes
Cook time: 30 minutes
Serves: 4–6

Tools:

- 1 medium saucepan
- Cutting board
- Knife
- Peeler or paring knife

Ingredients:

- 4 large Bosc pears
- ¼ cup (60 ml) maple syrup
- 1 large cinnamon stick
- 2 teaspoons cardamom pods, crushed with the back of a knife
- ¼ teaspoon vanilla extract
- 3 cups (750 ml) water
- Juice of 1 lemon or lime
- Coconut cream or non-dairy yogurt for serving
- A dash of ground cinnamon for garnish

Instructions:

1. Using a peeler or a paring knife, peel the pears.
2. Add the maple syrup, water, and juice into a pan and bring to a simmer over medium heat. Stir gently to combine everything.
3. Add in the peeled pears, cinnamon stick, cardamom pods, and vanilla extract to the simmering poaching liquid and reduce the temperature to medium-low.
4. Simmer, uncovered, for 20 minutes or until the pears are tender enough to slice through.
5. Remove pears with a slotted spoon.
6. Cut the pears in half to create more servings or leave them whole for a more dramatic presentation.
7. Serve with a dollop of coconut cream or over your favorite non-dairy yogurt. Garnish with a dash of ground cinnamon.

Stefanie Adler is a health and wellness professional and the founder of Bright Bean Health. She facilitates wellness retreats and events. Her work is focused on the intersection of physical and emotional well-being. After living abroad for several years, Stefanie moved to California where she enjoys the bounty of seasonal whole foods and her connection to the community. Stefanie enjoys cooking, reading, and spends as much time outside in nature as possible.

NAOMI

STORY

Born in the land of Israel, Naomi travels to Moab with her husband and sons to avoid a famine. While in Moab, her husband Elimelech dies. Her sons marry local women Orpah and Ruth, but die before having children.

Heartbroken, Naomi decides to return to Israel. To give her daughters-in-law the chance to have families and children, Naomi releases them of any obligation to her and sends them back to their families of origin. Orpah eventually tearfully concedes, but Ruth declares her commitment to remain with Naomi. The two women make the journey to Israel, where Naomi tells her neighbors to call her Mara, "bitter," rather than Naomi ("pleasantness"). Women alone, they must resort to gleaning – collecting fallen grain, in this case of the barley harvest – in surrounding fields. Naomi immediately recognizes the potential in Boaz, her cousin and the owner of the first field Ruth attempts to glean from.

Naomi orchestrates a plot using a strange custom of inheritance. The custom dictates that male relatives of a married man who died heirless may take over his property – but only by marrying his widow and designating their future children to inherit it. Boaz is relation enough to perform this act, and Naomi is concerned about Ruth's future happiness. And so Naomi coaches Ruth in how to quietly lie at his feet at night in the threshing room – an act of intimacy. Boaz, startled, finds Ruth under his blanket. She repeats what Naomi has taught her to say, explaining that he is the redeeming kinsman. Dispensing with a potential rival kinsman, Boaz claims Ruth as his wife. They have a son for whom Naomi cares as though he were her own – so much so that her neighbors proclaim, "A son is born to Naomi!" Her family line restored and Ruth's happiness assured, her story concludes.

VERSES

"And Naomi said, "Go back, my daughters, why should you go with me?…for it is far more bitter for me than for you because the LORD's hand has come out against me."

—Ruth 1:11–14

"And Naomi her mother-in-law said to her, "My daughter, shall I not seek for you a settled place for you, that it will be well for you? And now, is not Boaz our kinsmen with whose young women you were winnowing barley at the threshing floor tonight? And you must bathe and annoint yourself and put on your garments and go down to the threshing floor…and you shall come and uncover his feet and lie down, and as for him, he will tell you what to do."

—Ruth 3:1–4

"And the women said to Naomi, "Blessed is the LORD, Who has not deprived you of a redeemer today, and let his name be proclaimed in Israel. And may he be a restorer of life for you and a support for your old age, as your daughter-in-law, whom you love, has born him, who has been better to you than seven sons."

—Ruth 4:14–17

THEMES

Embitterment and Renewal

Naomi's story includes cycles of embitterment and renewal. This is reflected in her shifting fortune and in the changing of her name from Naomi to Mara and back. Her story of motherhood is also one of losses and regain, as she grieves her sons and gains a doting daughter-in-law, finally becoming a besotted grandmother to Obed.

Mothering

Naomi is a mother first to her biological children, then to Ruth, and finally to her grandson. Her willingness to share her maternal energy with Ruth even after her son has died is a key decision in her story. Rather than stagnate in isolation and grief, she repurposes her maternal love in devotion to her daughter-in-law, which in turn creates a fulfilling, loving second chapter for her own life.

MIDRASH

"And Ruth said: entreat me not to leave you and to return from following you" – what does "entreat" [lit. "hurt"] mean? Ruth said to Naomi, "Do not sin against me by telling me to leave and return from following you. I intend to convert anyway, and it is better that I do it with you than with someone else." When Naomi heard this, she immediately began to lay out before her the laws of conversion. Naomi said, "My daughter, Jewish women do not go to the non-Jews'

theaters and circuses." Ruth said, "Where you go, I will go." Naomi said, "My daughter, Jewish women do not live in a house where there is no mezuzah." Ruth said, "Where you lodge, I will lodge." "Your people shall be my people," refers to warning and punishment, and "Your God shall be my God" refers to the rest of the mitzvot.

—Ruth Rabbah 2:22

Naomi, even in the midst of her own profound personal pain and loss, maintains her connection with Judaism and the Jewish people. Her duty in the moment is to see to Ruth's Jewish education, so that Ruth's commitment to her and to the Jewish people is, at it were, kosher. It's worth noting that this passage expands Ruth's love and devotion, changing a personal declaration of loyalty to a single family, a single woman, into a metamorphosis.

This dialogue is imagined by the rabbis (a version also appears in the Babylonian Talmud, tractate *Yevamot*); the original text is opaque because the *TaNaKh* doesn't have as much of a framework for conversion. In reframing this conversation (in the original text, more of a monologue), it's not only Ruth's ambitions and motives that are magnified, sanctified, and redirected. Naomi, too, rather than remain a static creature who is silent in her grief, grudgingly accepting Ruth's commitment, becomes something of a heroine at this moment in the story as she is energized by her role in her daughter-in-law's Jewish education. The key in this exchange is that Ruth voiced her preference to learn with Naomi over anyone else. Naomi's special role as Ruth's Jewish teacher must have resonated with mothers-in-law across time.

PROMPTS

Naomi's story depends on two totally contradictory conceptions of family and obligation – her relationship with Ruth is model of obligation that arises from mutual affection, while Boaz views her as legal kin, and therefore his responsibility. How do we observe these two kinds of bonds at work in our own lives?

Is it right for Naomi to plot Boaz and Ruth's relationship? When is motherly meddling useful, or even necessary? When not?

Naomi tells her neighbors that she has returned "empty," only be reminded by them at the end of the megillah that her daughter-in-law loves her and is better than seven sons. How do we balance loss and grief with appreciation for the blessings left us?

How do faith and fortune affect one another? This story is full of reverses of fortune, and characters sometimes respond with anger towards God, or faith in other people, or with public declarations of Divine goodness. How have you experienced these phenomena in relation to one another?

Melanie Weiss is the Director of Summer Programs for the Center for Small Town Jewish Life, and the Director of Education at Beth Israel Congregation of Waterville, Maine. A graduate of Sarah Lawrence College, the Jewish Theological Seminary, and the Dorot Fellowship in Israel, she enjoys living in beautiful Maine with her wife and daughters.

SWEET MAPLE VEGETABLE BARLEY SALAD

We read the journey of Ruth and Naomi each year on the holiday of Shavuot. Barley and pomegranate are traditional foods that celebrate Shavuot and are two of the seven sacred foods to the land of Israel. This recipe features barley as Ruth meets Boaz during the barley harvest. The lightness of the herbs and lemon symbolizes the bright future they have together and the spring season of Shavuot.

This barley salad is simple to prepare and bursting with freshness. The bright flavor of the pomegranate works wonderfully with the nutty flavor from the barley. The carrots and the red onion round up the salad with a good dose of vitamins and a bit of crunch.

Prep time: 10 minutes
Cook time: 50 minutes
Serves: 4

Tools:

- Cutting board
- Sharp knife for cutting vegetables
- Box grater or grating peeler
- Tablespoon and teaspoon measuring cups
- Soup pot with a lid
- Large decorative bowl
- Serving spoon

Ingredients:

- 4 cups (400 g) cooked barley
- 1 pomegranate, seeded
- 1 red onion, chopped
- 2 carrots, shredded
- ¼ cup (10 g) fresh parsley or cilantro, chopped
- 1 lemon
- 1 tablespoon olive oil
- ½ teaspoon himalayan sea salt
- ¼ teaspoon cracked black pepper
- 1 tablespoon real maple syrup

Instructions:

1. Cook 2 cups (100 g) of dried pearl barley according to package instructions and set aside to cool down for a bit.
2. In a large salad bowl, add the red onion, carrots and fresh parsley. Gently mix the vegetables.
3. Squeeze the lemon juice into the bowl with the vegetables and add in the olive oil, maple syrup, salt and pepper. Toss the vegetables with the dressing.
4. Add the warm barley into the salad and let it soak in the dressing for 10–15 minutes.
5. Stir around ⅔ of the pomegranate seeds into the salad and serve garnished with the remaining pomegranate seeds.

Lily Aronin *is a holistic nutritionist, certified weight loss mentor, and mother of five. She offers one-to-one nutrition support and facilitates online challenges on sugar detox and plant-based eating. She encourages people to treat their bodies with kindness and to set reasonable nutrition and fitness goals.*

RUGELACH

These cookies are dedicated to the second phase of Naomi's life as a mother-in-law to Ruth and Boaz and a grandmother to their son Obed. Rugelach feels like the type of cookie that a grandmother would make and share with her family.

This classic cookie gets a plant-based, low-fat makeover. It is packed with sweet and nutty flavors from the jam, currants, and pecans. This cookie uses healthier ingredients, but keeps all of the original flavor at the same time. What could be better?

Prep time: 1 hour & 30 minutes

Cook time: 20 minutes

Serves: 4 dozen

Tools:

- 2 large mixing bowls
- Fork
- Optional: Electric mixer
- Plastic wrap
- Small bowl
- Spatula
- Pizza cutter
- 2 Large baking sheets (with edges)
- Parchment paper
- Wire cooling/baking rack

Ingredients:

For the dough:

- 2 ¼ cups (290 g) all-purpose flour (or gluten-free all-purpose flour) + extra for rolling out
- ¼ cup (30 g) arrowroot flour
- ½ teaspoon sea salt
- ¼ cup (60 g) sugar
- 1 cup (200 g) white bean puree
- ½ cup (125 g) Earth Balance, softened
- ¼ cup (75 g) applesauce
- ¼ cup (60 g) tahini

For the filling:

- ½ cup (120 g) sugar (preferably unrefined)
- ½ cup (165 g) all-fruit raspberry or apricot jam
- 1 cup (125 g) pecans, finely chopped and toasted
- ¾ cup (115 g) currants
- 1 ½ teaspoons ground cinnamon
- Powdered sugar for dusting (or you can brush with a little non-dairy milk and sprinkle with sugar before baking)

Instructions:

1. Prepare the dough the night before you plan to bake the cookies. In a large mixing bowl, whisk together the all-purpose flour, arrowroot flour, sea salt, and sugar. At this point you can finish preparing the dough either by hand or using an electric mixer with large paddle attachments.

2. Make the bean puree. Drain and rinse a can of white beans (navy beans or cannellini beans) and rinse them in a strainer a few times with cold water. Place them in a mini food processor and process until smooth. Use 1 cup for this recipe. You will have leftover bean puree.

3. To finish the dough by hand: In another large bowl, mix together the white bean puree, Earth Balance, applesauce, and tahini. Add the flour mixture to the bean mixture and combine with a fork until a smooth dough forms.

4. To make the dough with an electric mixer: add the white bean puree, Earth Balance, applesauce, and tahini in the bowl of an electric mixer fitted with the paddle attachment and beat until light. Add the flour mixture and mix just until a soft dough forms.

5. Transfer the dough onto a floured board and roll into a ball. Cut the ball into 4 equal pieces. Shape the pieces into 4 balls and flatten into 4 disks. Wrap each disk and refrigerate overnight.

6. To prepare and bake the cookies, preheat the oven to 350°F (180°C) degrees.

7. In a small bowl, mix together the sugar, jam, pecans, currants and cinnamon.

8. Unwrap one of the disks of chilled dough. On a floured surface and using a floured rolling pin, roll out the dough into a 9-inch (22 cm) circle. Using a spatula, carefully transfer the rolled out dough to a piece of parchment paper and return to the refrigerator. Repeat with the remaining disks of dough.

9. Remove a circle of dough from the refrigerator and spread with ¼ of the nut-jam mixture. Work quickly so that the dough remains cold.

10. Using a pizza cutter, cut the circle into 12 equal wedges. First, cut the circle into 4 quarters, then cut each quarter into three pieces. Roll up each wedge starting from the wide side, into a crescent shape. Place the cookie on the parchment lined baking sheet, with the point tucked under. Repeat with remaining prepared wedges. If the dough seems to have softened you can refrigerate the prepared cookies for 25 minutes before baking. The chilling helps to create a crisper cookie texture.

11. Bake rugelach until lightly browned, around 20 minutes. Remove to a wire rack and cool. Repeat with remaining chilled dough and filling.

12. Serve dusted with powdered sugar.

From the Jewish Food Hero Kitchen

RUTH

STORY

Ruth, a Moabite woman, is one of two women to have her own book of the *TaNaKh, Megillat Ruth*. Her persistence, strength and vigor make her story of love, loss and redemption a source of inspiration. Ruth is known as the first individual requesting to convert.

Ruth was married to Mahlon, one of the sons of Naomi and Elimelech, who had moved to Moab during a time of famine in Bethlehem. Ruth, Naomi and Ruth's sister-in-law, Orpah, all become childless widows while living in Moab. When Naomi decides to return home to her family in Bethlehem, both her daughters-in-law try to go with her. Naomi spurns them, repeating "Go back to your people" three times, insisting they should return to their own mothers and remarry. Orpah leaves, but Ruth remains steadfast and issues an unequivocal statement "wherever you go, I will go... your people will be my people and your God my God." This portion of the story of Ruth is cited as one of the reasons for the older tradition rejecting an individual requesting conversion three times.

Upon returning to Bethlehem, Ruth gleans in the wheat and barley fields to sustain her mother-in-law and herself. She gleans in the fields of Boaz, a relative of her deceased husband who admires her loyalty and kindness to Naomi. She eventually marries Boaz, thus preserving Naomi's family name. Boaz and Ruth have a son, Obed. Through Obed's son, Ruth becomes the Great-grandmother of David, Israel's greatest king.

Due to her statement of love and loyalty, Ruth is considered the first convert to Judaism.

VERSES

"And Ruth said, "Do not entreat me to forsake you, to turn back from you. For wherever you go, I will go. And wherever you lodge, I will lodge. Your people is my people, and your god is my god."

—Ruth 1:16

"And Ruth the Moabite said to Naomi, "Let me go, pray, to the field, and glean from among the ears of grain after I find favor in his eyes." And she said to her, "Go, my daughter." And she went and came and gleaned in the field behind the reapers, and it chanced that she came upon the plot of Boaz, who was from the clan of Elimelech."

—Ruth 2:2–3

"And Boaz answered and said, "It was indeed told me, all that you did for your mother-in-law after your husband's death, and that you left your mother and father in the land of your birth to come to a people that you did not know in the past."

—Ruth 2:11

THEMES

Loyalty

After Naomi rebuffs Ruth's request to accompany her to Bethlehem, Ruth insists and refuses to abandon her mother in law, vowing to God to always stay with Naomi. Once they have reached Bethlehem, Ruth continues to care for Naomi, going out to the fields during the harvest season to gather grain in order for them to eat. Ruth's devotion serves as a model of caring for family, however that family is defined.

Kindness

There is much kindness and consideration for the well-being of others throughout this short book. Ruth, Naomi and Boaz all show kindness and care for each other. Throughout this story, each individual has opportunities to reject or humiliate the other. They choose not to. They each exhibit a gentle forbearance and patience for the other. By doing this they elevate their relationships, creating new opportunities as their paths move forward.

Bravery

Ruth started the story as a childless widow and ends triumphant, by being willing to embrace change. She could have returned to the known safety of her family and instead she chose to move to a new land where her people were disliked. Once in Bethlehem, she chose not to hide inside, instead heading to the fields for the backbreaking work of gleaning. She followed her mother in law's advice in approaching Boaz as she sought redemption and independence for them both. She did not resign herself to her situation as a childless widow, but found strength and proved herself to be a courageous and determined immigrant. She won a place for herself, forging a reputation of kindness and loyalty, respected amongst her new people.

MIDRASH

Rabbi Zeira says, "This scroll (Megillat Ruth) does not have anything in it concerned with impurity or purity nor what is forbidden and what is permitted. So why is it written? To teach us the greatness of the reward for acts of loving kindness."

—*Ruth Rabbah* 2:14

Ruth's story of strength, courage and daring is underpinned by care for the other. Each individual is presented with choices and each time, chooses kindness.

Even though Naomi is embittered upon her return to Bethlehem, she does not take Ruth's company for granted. She does not humiliate Ruth for being childless, strongly stigmatised at that time. Instead she looks for ways to secure Ruth's future.

Ruth is alone and friendless in a new land, but pursues a path to support her beloved mother-in-law. Ruth goes to the fields, knowing that, as a widow without a family to protect her, she may be harrassed. As noted later, Ruth does not seek out the companionship of men, but returns home to Naomi.

Boaz does not abuse his power over Ruth or Naomi but seeks to protect them, telling his workers to leave extra grain for Ruth to collect. When Ruth surprises Boaz on the threshing floor – a woman in a place where she should not be – he does not take advantage of her. Instead, he reacts with kindness, agreeing to the marriage plan and sending Ruth home with additional grain before she can be seen by others.

The theme of familial relations in Ruth's story resonates across time. Families can be chosen not just born into, as Ruth did with Naomi and Boaz. When times are rough, as difficult as it might be, choosing to make a habit of showing and voicing kindness reaps rewards.

PROMPTS

What was a specific time in your life when others discouraged you? Did you submit or continue, knowing your path was worth the cost?

Is there a relationship you'd leave everything for? Is it reciprocal? Does reciprocity matter?

Describe a time when you have been strengthened by joining forces with other women?

How do you show loving kindness to either your biological or chosen family?

Edith Yakutis *is a second career rabbinic student at Hebrew Union College-Jewish Institute of Religion. Prior to starting her studies, she worked for 22 years at Microsoft Corporation as a Team Manager for development teams and the Account Manager for a number of Fortune 100 companies. She and her husband, Leo, founded Temple Solel in Fort Mill, SC, along with 11 other families. She served there as lay leader prior to moving to Cincinnati, Ohio and starting her rabbinic studies. She is a passionate home cook and challah baker.*

VEGAN FLUFFY CHALLAH

Ruth can be described as a woman who embodies chesed. Chesed is difficult to translate as it has no precise English equivalent. It connotes loyalty, compassion, generosity, goodness, kindness, and steadfast love. Its ultimate manifestation is performing mitzvot with purity of virtue or lack of motive, in other words: "something for nothing". To me challah is symbolic of chesed.

As a convert to Judaism, the story of Ruth and making challah have personal resonance for me. My Jewish home is enhanced on Shabbat with the kneading, blessing and nourishment of challah. Just as water aids the dough in rising to its full potential, water also brings life to all things and represents the attribute of chesed.

This vegan challah is soft, fluffy, and delicious. It has just the right amount of sweetness for a treat for weekend brunch, served with jam and a tall cup of coffee.

Prep time: 6 hours
Cook time: 30 minutes
Serves: 2 large loaves

Tools:

- Large prep bowl
- Dough scraper
- Silpat or other non-stick silicone mat for even baking
- Dry measuring cups
- Baking tray
- Mixing spoon or rubber spatula

Ingredients:

- 8 cups (1 kg) unbleached, all-purpose flour (start with less flour and add only as needed)
- ¾ cup (180 ml) organic canola oil (or vegetable oil)
- 1 cup (200 g) ultra fine baker's sugar
- 2 ½ cups (625 ml) warm water
- 1 ½ tablespoons salt
- 3 packets (3 tablespoons or 25 g) yeast
- Sweet soy milk

Instructions:

1. In a large bowl, combine sugar, water, yeast, and oil. Stir and allow yeast to work and bubble for 10 minutes.

2. Add the salt and 7 cups (900 g) of flour. Stir well and transfer the mixture onto a clean, lightly floured surface.

3. Knead the dough for 10 minutes, gradually adding from the remaining flour, only as needed, to make the dough less sticky.

4. Lightly grease a deep bowl and place the dough in the bowl, turning it gently so all sides are nicely greased – this prevents the dough from forming a crust. Cover the bowl with a damp cloth.

5. Allow to rise for about two hours or until the dough doubles in volume.

6. Punch down the dough and allow it to rise for a second time, about another hour.

7. Transfer the dough onto a lightly floured surface. Divide the dough into three equal parts and form into large strands. Braid the three strands together. Divide the braid into 2 loaves.

8. Preheat your oven to 350°F (180°C) degrees.

9. Allow the braided challah to rise for another 20–30 minutes before transferring into the pre-heated oven for 20 minutes. After 20 minutes, take the challah out of the oven and baste with sweet soy milk, then place back in the oven for another 10 minutes, or until golden-brown.

10. Let the challah cool completely before slicing and serving.

Joan Laguatan is a Filipina-Jewish mom and real-estate broker. She was born in the Philippines and grew up and lives in San Francisco. She is passionate about veganism (she and her husband had a vegan wedding), and she hosts an annual "compassionate" vegan Passover seder. She enjoys making challah for her family and others for Shabbat.

ISRAELI VEGGIE COUSCOUS WITH "POPCORN" CAULIFLOWER AND SWEET CHILI SAUCE

The Hebrew Bible uses the word 'hometz'- vinegar in modern Hebrew – to describe the dip enjoyed at the meal Ruth shared with Boaz the day they met. Some interpretations prefer to translate this as "hummus," an infinitely more appetizing dish to dip one's bread in. This meal is one I like to think would have sustained Ruth as she set out for a long day sowing the harvest.

As a nod to their first shared meal, this dish of Israeli couscous is studded with chickpeas that have been soaked, boiled, and then roasted in the oven alongside a colorful display of sweet potato and red onion. Supplemented by a side dish of beer battered, baked, panko-coated cauliflower florets, and homemade, Thai-style sweet chili dipping sauce that is both less spicy, and easier to whip up than it would seem, this complete meal is a filling plant-based alternative for the Shavuot holiday – a holiday otherwise marked by way too much cheesecake.

Prep time: 45 minutes

Cook time: 1 hour

Serves: 4–6

Tools:

- Large Pot
- Whisk
- Small pot
- Rubber gloves

- Chef's knife
- Paring knife
- Chopping board
- Fine mesh strainer
- Oven tray and baking paper
- 2 medium bowls
- Measuring spoons/cups (if desired)
- Wooden spoon
- Large mixing bowl

Ingredients:

For the cous cous:

- 1 cup (165 g) canned chickpeas, rinsed and drained
- 2 medium red onions, chopped
- 1 small sweet potato, chopped
- 1–2 tablespoons high-quality olive oil
- 1 cup (140 gr) Israeli couscous, uncooked
- 1–2 tablespoons high-quality olive oil
- salt and pepper to taste

For the sweet chili dipping sauce:

- 1 heaping tablespoon cornstarch
- 2 tablespoons water
- 1 red chili pepper, finely chopped
- 5 garlic cloves, crushed
- ¼ cup plus 1 tablespoon (75ml) rice wine vinegar
- ¾ cup (280ml) water
- 1 cup (200 g) white sugar

- 2 tablespoons plus 1 teaspoon soy sauce
- For the "popcorn" cauliflower:
- 2.2 lb. (1kg) whole cauliflower, broken down into florets
- 10 oz. (300ml) beer
- 1 cup (120 g) flour
- ½ teaspoon salt
- Pinch granulated garlic/black pepper/paprika
- 2 ¼ cups (110 grams) panko bread crumbs
- ¼ teaspoon salt, or more to taste
- Olive oil for drizzling

Instructions:

1. Preheat your oven to 350°F (180°C) degrees and line two large baking sheets with a piece of parchment paper.

2. To make the popcorn cauliflower, prepare the beer batter by whisking together flour and spices in a medium-sized bowl. Slowly pour in beer and whisk until smooth.

3. Dip each cauliflower floret into the beer batter mixture and then dip into the panko crumbs one at a time, making sure to coat each nook and cranny with the crumbs.

4. Place breaded cauliflower on one of the prepared baking sheets, drizzle with a small amount of olive oil, and bake until golden and crisp on the outside, and nicely soft and tender on the inside, around 50–60 minutes.

5. Add the onions, sweet potato, and chickpeas to the second prepared baking sheet and drizzle with olive oil. Toss to coat the vegetables and chickpeas and season with salt and pepper to taste. Roast until the sweet potatoes are fork-tender, around 30 minutes.

6. While the vegetables are roasting, prepare the Israeli couscous according to package directions. Set aside to cool.

7. In the meantime, in a small bowl combine cornstarch with 2 tablespoons water. Mix with a fork until smooth. Set aside.

8. In a medium saucepan, combine rice wine vinegar, water, sugar, and soy sauce. Bring to a light boil, then reduce to a gentle simmer.

9. Add in the chili pepper, garlic, and cornflour and water mixture. Continue to simmer for 2–5 minutes, or until thickened to a syrupy consistency.

10. Let the sweet chili dip cool down then store in the fridge where it will keep for up to 2 weeks.

11. To assemble, in a large bowl, combine the sweet potato and chickpea mixture with the Israeli couscous. Drizzle with another 2–3 tablespoons of olive oil and season with salt and pepper to taste. Serve alongside popcorn cauliflower and sweet chili sauce.

Jessica Halfin is an Israeli-trained baker, gourmet cook, recipe developer, and widely published food writer. She is a regular contributor to, among others, Hadassah Magazine. She currently resides in the Northern Israeli city of Haifa with her husband and three small boys, where she can be found baking, preserving, and pushing the boundaries of what can be made from scratch.

ESTHER

STORY

Esther is an unlikely hero. She saves the Jewish communities across the Persian Empire through her wit, courage, and cunning. After Esther was orphaned as a young girl, her uncle Mordechai adopted her. He was a proud Jew, uncompromising in his beliefs, and also an important ally to King Ahashverosh.

When Queen Vashti was banished from the palace for defying the King's drunken and humiliating orders, a beauty contest was held to find the next queen. Esther was chosen to be the king's next wife, although no one in the palace knew she was Jewish.

Esther is called upon to overcome her fears when Ahashverosh's advisor, Haman, plots to kill all of the Jewish people in Persia. Her uncle, Mordechai, famously tells her that her silence will not save her, and that she rose to this position of power, perhaps, precisely to serve as her people's savior. She must defy protocol, gender norms, and established power dynamics to reveal her Jewish identity and plead with the king to save her people. Esther's courage and skillful engagement with the king works. She saves the Jewish people and sets the stage for the punishment of their enemies.

Each Purim we tell her story and honor her courage.

VERSES

"For if indeed you remain silent, relief and rescue will come to the Jews from elsewhere and you and your father's house will perish. And who knows whether for just a time like this you have attained royalty?"

—Esther 4:13–14

"Go, assemble all the Jews who are in Shushan, and fast on my behalf, and do not eat or drink three days, night and day. And I, too, with my young women, shall fast in this fashion. And so, I shall come to the king not according to rule, and if I perish, I perish."

—Esther 4:16

"And Queen Esther answered and said, "If I have found favor in the eyes of the king, and if it please the king, let my life be granted me in my petition and my people's in my request."

—Esther 7:3

THEMES

Courage

Esther was clear-sighted about the risks to her safety when she spoke out against Haman's evil plot. Courage is not ignoring the risks of speaking out, it is knowing the risks involved and speaking out for the sake of our spiritual and physical survival.

Identification

Anti-semitism is one of the most ancient hatreds that we still experience today. It rarely serves us to be public about our Jewish identities in non-Jewish spaces. Esther voluntarily forgoes the privilege of her hiddenness and makes her Jewishness apparent. She teaches us to be authentic, proud, and upright in the face of bigotry.

Strategy

Esther finds ways to achieve her aims within a system replete with misogyny and antisemitism. Sometimes we must work in unjust systems in order to survive and move our community forward. Esther shows skill in playing within existing systems to save her people, even when it is not easy or fair. The ability to strategize in a variety of contexts is a key component in effective leadership, even when one recognizes the flaws within such contexts.

MIDRASH

If you are silent now and do not defend your people, you will end up staying silent in the future and you will have no excuse. Why? Because you could have done good in your lifetime and you did not. Do you think that God will abandon the Jewish people? In any case he will bring a redeemer for Israel.

—Esther Rabbah 8:6

Esther could have stayed silent. She could have stayed *nesteret*, hidden among the radical threats coming from Ahaverosh's inner circle. She could have protected herself, at least temporarily, from the fate of her exposed sisters and brothers. Just as Moses chose to forfeit his privilege and position to fight for justice among his people, so too Esther chose to put her comfort and safety on the line to fight for her people's survival and dignity.

כִּי אִם־הַחֲרֵשׁ תַּחֲרִישִׁי בָּעֵת הַזֹּאת רֶוַח וְהַצָּלָה יַעֲמוֹד לַיְּהוּדִים מִמָּקוֹם אַחֵר וְאַתְּ וּבֵית־אָבִיךְ תֹּאבֵדוּ וּמִי יוֹדֵעַ אִם־לְעֵת
כָּזֹאת הִגַּעַתְּ לַמַּלְכוּת:

"On the contrary, if you keep silent in this crisis, relief and deliverance will come to the Jews from another quarter, while you and your father's house will perish. And who knows, perhaps you have attained power for just such a crisis."

—Esther 4:14

When Esther was gripped by fear, when her voice shook, she did not cling to fleeting privilege and the illusion of safety. Her power and privilege had a purpose: to protect those who could not protect themselves. Esther is the foremother who teaches us the power of privilege leveraged well. She did not hide, or feel guilty, or ignore the greater context of her world. She used her position to save lives and bring the wicked to justice.

This is the lesson I learn from our most majestic ancestor: do not run from power. Grasp it with both hands and use it wisely, strategically, and strongly. Our national and global futures depend on it.

PROMPTS

When have you been courageous, and what made those moments special?

When do you reveal yourself as a Jew, and when do you keep it hidden? Why? What other parts of your identity do you selectively reveal, and why?

Vashti and Esther represent two modes of resistance against structural injustice. Vashti confronted injustice in a public and defiant way. Esther was strategic and private in her appeals for justice. How do you balance the value and applicability of both modes of resistance?

Mordechai was an important mentor for Esther in finding the courage to speak out despite the risks involved. Who are the people in your life that sustain and strengthen you when you need the courage to speak out.

Rabbi Rachel Isaacs is the spiritual leader of Beth Israel Congregation in Waterville, Maine and a professor of Jewish Studies at Colby College. She also directs the Center for Small Town Jewish Life at Colby. She lives in central Maine with her wife and two daughters.

PERSIAN CARROT JAM (MORABA YE HAVEEJ)

The decadent Persian feasting is a recurring setting in Esther's story as she uses her feasts to communicate with her husband and triumph over the evil Haman. To this end, I chose to make a rich and bright Persian recipe, Moraba ye Haveej, a sweet and savory carrot jam that is fit for a queen and her table.

This recipe uses carrots, rather than a fruit or berry. Carrots give a beautiful texture and bring a healthy dose of vitamin C and beta carotene. This is a recipe that can be canned and used year round as a punchy jam or accompaniment to salty cheeses or flatbreads. This jam can be used as a sweet and savory hamantaschen filling.

Prep time: 10 minutes

Cook time: 30 minutes

Serves: 4 medium-sized pots of jam, about 8 oz. (230 g) each

Tools:

- Medium-sized pot
- Wooden spoon
- Kitchen scale
- Measuring spoons
- Box grater

Ingredients:

- 1.1 lbs. (500 g) organic carrots, peeled and finely grated
- 1 ¾ cups (350 g) cassonade sugar
- 1 ½ cups (375 ml) water
- 1 ½ cups (375 ml) orange juice
- 1 tablespoon lemon juice
- 4 cardamom pods, ground
- Pinch of cinnamon
- 1 tablespoon rose or orange blossom water

Instructions:

1. Add grated carrots, cassonade sugar, water, orange juice, cardamom, and cinnamon to a medium pot and stir well to incorporate.
2. Place the pot over low heat and let the jam slowly cook away. It is important to use low heat and slowly warm the jam at the beginning, to prevent sugar crystals from forming during cooling.
3. Once the sugar is melted, increase the temperature to medium/medium high and bring the jam to a gentle boil. At first, the consistency will be rather thin and liquidy.
4. Continue cooking, letting the carrots cook through and the liquid reduce.
5. When the carrots have become darker and slightly translucent and the mixture reaches to a jam-like texture, stir in a spoonful of rose or orange blossom water.
6. Place the jam in sanitized jars for canning, or any sealable container to store in the fridge. Store canned jam in a cool, dark closet or uncanned jam in the fridge.

Laurel Beth Kratochvila is originally from Sharon, Massachusetts. She is a Cordon Bleu trained boulangère who has worked the baguette lines in Paris bakeries. She puts her skills to use at her Berlin bakery, Fine Bagels, where she serves up all the treats of a traditional Yiddish bakery. She is committed to promoting and preserving Jewish food culture through Nosh Berlin Jewish food events, bakery workshops, and recipe development.

PERSIAN LENTIL RICE WITH SAFFRON, ROASTED PUMPKIN, CRISPY ONIONS, AND DATES

One aspect of observant Jewish life which Esther was not afforded in the palace was kosher meat. Thus, Jewish tradition explains that Queen Esther took it upon herself to eat plant-based during her time in the palace, where she was consequently fed seeds and legumes.

A staple in Persian cuisine, the humble lentils are packed with fiber, plant-based protein, iron, and magnesium. Combined with the fragrant saffron rice, sweet dates, chewy sultanas, and crispy onions, they make for a meal that satisfies all senses.

Prep time: 15 minutes

Cook time: 1 hour & 30 minutes

Serves: 6–8

Tools:

- Chopping board
- Sharp knife
- Measuring spoons
- Large mixing bowl
- Spatula
- Wooden spoon
- Sieve
- Large pot
- Heavy bottomed saucepan with lid
- Pastry brush
- Small bowl
- Round serving platter
- Oven mittens
- Dishtowel

Ingredients:

- 1 Kent pumpkin, peeled and cubed
- 4–5 medium brown onions, diced
- 1 15-oz. (400 g) can brown lentils, rinsed and drained
- ½ cup (100 g) golden raisins
- ½ cup (100 g) medjool dates, quartered lengthwise
- 3 cups (400 g) basmati rice, rinsed and drained
- 2 tablespoons Persian Advieh spice blend
- 2 tablespoons salt
- 1 cup (250 ml) water for onions
- 3 cups (750ml) water to cook the rice
- 4–5 tablespoons extra-virgin olive oil

Instructions:

1. Preheat your oven to 350°F (180°C) degrees.

2. Place cubed pumpkin on a parchment-lined baking tray and brush with approximately 1 tablespoon of olive oil and season with salt to taste. Bake until the pumpkin is lightly browned and fork-tender, around 30 minutes.

3. Meanwhile, add the onions to a small saucepan and pour in 1 cup of water. Place over medium heat and cook, stirring occasionally, for 20–25 minutes.

4. Once the water has almost fully evaporated and the onions are translucent, add a tablespoon of olive oil and reduce the heat to low. Continue cooking until the onions become golden and caramelised, around 15–20 minutes.

5. Add the Advieh spice mix and cook for another 1–2 minutes.

6. Add the drained lentils, golden raisins, and medjool dates and cook for another 2–3 minutes. Season with salt to taste and remove from heat. Set aside.

7. To prepare the rice, pour 3 cups of water in a medium pot and bring to a full boil. Add in the rice and cover with a lid. Cook until the rice is barely cooked, around 9–10 minutes. Remove from heat and rinse the rice under cold water.

8. In the same pot you used for the rice, heat two tablespoons of olive oil and add in the onion-lentil-raisin-date mix, baked pumpkin, and rice.

9. Using the back of a wooden spoon, dome the rice into a conical shape and using the handle, poke several holes (almost reaching the bottom of the pot) into the rice. Replace the lid, putting a clean tea towel under it to ensure steam doesn't escape. Cook on a low heat for approximately 15 minutes.

10. Remove the lid, redome the rice, and drizzle olive oil around the perimeter of the pot. Increase the heat to medium, cover with a lid, and cook for another 3 minutes.

11. When ready, the rice will make popping and crackling noises and smell fragrant and toasted. It should come away from the sides and bottom of the pot with no resistance, indicating that the crispy crust has formed.

12. Place a serving dish directly on top of the pot and wearing oven mitts or using tea towels, swiftly and confidently flip over the rice, like turning a cake out of its pan. Gently remove the pot and serve immediately.

Lainie Cadry is a newly registered nurse and holds a New Graduate position at the Sydney Children's Hospital in Sydney, Australia. Lainie's cooking is influenced by her passion for health and her diverse Jewish cultural heritage from Persia and Eastern Europe. At 20 years old, Lainie was the youngest contributor published in the Monday Morning Cooking Club's third cookbook, "It's Always About the Food". Lainie runs a kosher food Instagram account named Lainie's Kitchen, where she reimagines traditional recipes with a fun, nourishing and soulful approach.

REFERENCES

All biblical verses quoted are from Robert Alter's translation of the Hebrew Bible, a three-volume work called *The Hebrew Bible: A Translation with Commentary*. We have provided page numbers of the biblical quotes here so that you can look them up and read them in their larger context. The book is available at university libraries, bookstores and can be purchased on Amazon.

Please see Alter, Robert, *The Hebrew Bible: A Translation with Commentary*, W.W. Norton & Company (2018).

Eve
Alter, Vol. 1, 15–19

Sarah
Alter, Vol. 1, 41–42, 57–58, 68

Hagar
Alter, Vol. 1, 52, 69–70

Rebekah
Alter, Vol. 1, 79–80, 84, 86–87

Rachel
Alter, Vol. 1, 104, 106, 109, 133

Leah
Alter, Vol. 1, 103–104, 106–108

Dinah
Alter, Vol. 1, 126–128, 130

Tamar
Alter, Vol. 1, 148–149, Vol. 3, 639

Shifra
Alter, Vol. 1, 215–216

Zipporah
Alter, Vol. 1, 219, 228–229, 286–287

Miriam
Alter, Vol. 1, 216–217, 277, 546

Rahab
Alter, Vol. 2, 11–13, 23–24

Deborah
Alter, Vol. 2, 94–95, 98

Yael
Alter, Vol. 2, 94–97

Hannah
Alter, Vol. 2, 178–180

Abigail
Alter, Vol. 2, 282, 284–285

Woman of Shunem
Alter, Vol. 2, 538–539, 540

Naomi
Alter, Vol. 3, 626, 632, 638

Ruth
Alter, Vol. 3, 627–630

Esther
Alter, Vol. 3, 728–729, 734

A NOTE ON INCLUSION

When I set out to create this project, my goal was a multicultural / multiethnic Jewish community vegan cookbook.

The Jewish women featured in this book live in the United States, England, Israel, Australia, Germany, Spain and Cambodia. Included are converts, Reform, Reconstructionist, Conservative and Orthodox Jews, women of African-American, Syrian and Asian backgrounds and women born in interfaith marriages. The ages of the women featured range from 9 years old to over 80 years old.

Going forward I will be continuing my efforts of Jewish inclusiveness and diversity in future projects. I would appreciate your help with this. Please contact me to submit recipes, be interviewed and featured on the blog. Please nominate amazing cooks and writers to contribute a recipe or a food story. Write to me at kenden@jewishfoodhero.com.

ACKNOWLEDGEMENTS

To each woman and girl who contributed to this book: thank you for trusting me enough to say yes to participate in this project. Each of you donated your intellectual labor for this community project that seeks to uplift the voices of women and promote healthy plant-based food in our community.

Thank you to Turner Publishing colleagues Stephanie Beard and Heather Howell for believing in this book project and responding to my questions and concerns throughout the project.

Rabbi Rachel Issacs and Melanie Weiss, your support for this project was so helpful to me at the beginning because you validated my idea. Had you been the leaders of the Beth Israel Jewish community when I was growing up in Central Maine, I would be a different Jewish woman today.

Thank you to Hebrew Union College colleagues Jean Bloch Rosensaft, Rabbi Dvora Weisberg, and Nancy Lewitt. Each of you sent out multiple emails inviting interested female Rabbinical and cantorial students to participate in this project. That active support facilitated the inclusion of student voices in this book.

Thank you to Mara Lassner at Ramaz School for helping me engage two thoughtful young Jewish women in high school and middle school who contributed to this project.

Thank you to Monica Kempler for sharing her mother Nora's recipe and helping me connect with the Melbourne Jewish community. Thank you for hosting us for Passover in Melbourne.

Bonny Coombe, your intellectual and copy editing support were essential. I will always remember the we spent together on this project as the beginning our friendship and a series of mornings when we drank too much coffee at Kinyei Cafe.

Hadassah Levy, thank you for sharing your religious knowledge with me. Your editing and content feedback gave me a lot of comfort throughout this entire project. I value that I always leave our conversations knowing more about Judaism.

To my Mother and Father, for your encouragement. Thank you for being open to new food and Shabbat dinners.

Charles, Merci d'avoir soutenu ce projet et de m'avoir appris tant de choses sur la persévérance et de rester concentré sur les "bénéficiaires".

ACKNOWLEDGEMENTS

Yaël, thank you for contributing your popsicle recipe and for drawing a picture of the Jewish Food Hero. You are the Jewish girl who inspires me to create and I hope you will cherish this book as a Jewish woman.

The Jewish Food Hero
by Yaël Alfond-Vincent

INDEX

CPSIA information can be obtained
at www.ICGtesting.com
Printed in the USA
BVHW020931180220
572678BV00010B/41